Citizenship and Ethnic Conflict

Making a case for separating citizenship from nationality, this book comparatively examines a selection of nation-states in terms of their definitions of nationality and citizenship, and the way in which the association of some with the European Union has transformed these definitions.

In a combination of case studies from Europe and the Middle East, this book's comparative framework addresses the question of citizenship and ethnic conflict from the foundation of the nation-state to the current challenges raised by globalization. This edited volume examines six different countries and looks at the way that ethnic or religious identity lies at the core of the national community, ultimately determining the state's definition and treatment of its citizens. The selected contributors to this new volume investigate this common ambiguity in the construction of nations, and look at the contrasting ways in which the issues of citizenship and identity are handled by different nation-states.

This book will be of great interest to students and scholars studying in the areas of citizenship and the nation-state, ethnic conflict, globalization, and Middle Eastern and European Politics.

Haldun Gülalp is Professor of Political Sociology at Yıldız Technical University in Istanbul, Turkey.

T0352767

Routledge Research in Comparative Politics

Citizenship and Ethnic Conflict

Challenging the nation-state

Edited by Haldun Gülalp

 Routledge
Taylor & Francis Group

LONDON AND NEW YORK

First published 2006
by Routledge
2 Park Square, Milton Park, Abingdon, Oxon OX14 4RN

Simultaneously published in the USA and Canada
by Routledge
270 Madison Ave, New York, NY10016

Routledge is an imprint of the Taylor & Francis Group

Transferred to Digital Printing 2009

Typeset in Sabon by
Bookcraft Ltd, Stroud, Gloucestershire

British Library Cataloguing in Publication Data
A catalogue record for this book is available from the
British Library

Library of Congress Cataloging in Publication Data
Gülalp, Haldun, 1951–
    Citizenship and ethnic conflict : challenging the nation-
state/ Haldun Gülalp. – 1st ed.
    p. cm. – (Routledge research in comparative politics)
    Includes bibliographical references and index.
    1. Citizenship. 2. Ethnic conflict. 3. Citizenship–Europe
Case studies. 4. Citizenship–Middle East–Case studies.
    5. Ethnic conflict–Europe–Case studies. 6. Ethnic conflict–
Middle East–Case studies. 7. National state.
    I. Title. II. Series.
    JF801.G85 2006
    323.6'094–dc22   2005013152

ISBN10: 0-415-36897-9 (hbk)
ISBN10: 0-415-49956-9 (pbk)

ISBN13: 978-0-415-36897-1 (hbk)
ISBN13: 978-0-415-49956-9 (pbk)

Contents

Notes on contributors

Soner Cagaptay is Senior Fellow and Director of the Turkish Research Program at the Washington Institute for Near East Policy in Washington, DC. He holds a PhD in history from Yale University (2003) and has received numerous grants, including Smith-Richardson, Mellon, Rice, and Leylan Fellowships.

Alain Dieckhoff is Senior Research Fellow at the CNRS (the French National Center for Scientific Research) and teaches at the Institute for Political Studies in Paris. He is the author of *L'invention d'une nation: Israel et la modernité politique* (1993) and *La nation dans tous ses Etats. Les identités nationales en mouvement* (2000).

Effie Fokas holds a PhD in political sociology from the London School of Economics. She is currently Research Fellow at the Hellenic Foundation for European and Foreign Policy (ELIAMEP) in Athens, and co-Director of its Forum for Interdisciplinary Study of Muslim–Christian Relations in Twenty-first Century Europe. She is also Research Associate at Exeter University, UK, and member of a research consortium studying Welfare and Religion in a European Perspective.

Haldun Gülalp is Professor of Political Sociology at Yıldız Technical University in Istanbul, Turkey. He is the author, most recently, of *Kimlikler Siyaseti: Türkiye'de Siyasal Islamin Temelleri* [*Politics of Identities: Foundations of Political Islam in Turkey*] (2003).

Riva Kastoryano is Senior Research Fellow at the CNRS (the French National Center for Scientific Research) and teaches at the Institute for Political Studies in Paris. She is the author of *La France, l'Allemagne et leurs immigrés: négocier l'identité* (1997).

Maurus Reinkowski is Professor of Islamic Studies at Freiburg University in Germany. He has been a Research Fellow at the Van Leer Jerusalem Institute and the Orient Institute Istanbul, and taught as Assistant Professor of Ottoman History in the Department of Turkish Languages and Cultures at the University of Bamberg, Germany. He is the author of *Filastin, Filistin und Eretz Israel: die späte osmanische Herrschaft über Palästina in der arabischen, türkischen und israelischen Historiographie* (1995).

Sofia Saadeh earned her PhD at Harvard University in 1974 and subsequently taught at the Lebanese–American University, the American University of Beirut, and the Lebanese University. Currently an Advisor to the Lebanese Deputy Prime Minister, Mr Issam Fares, she has authored *The Social Structure of Lebanon: Democracy or Servitude?* (1993), and *Antun Saadeh and Democracy in Geographic Syria* (2000).

Sami Zubaida is Emeritus Professor of Politics and Sociology, Birkbeck College, University of London. He is the author of *Islam, the People and the State* (1993) and *Law and Power in the Islamic World* (2003).

Acknowledgements

The idea for this book, though not the book itself, grew out of a conference that took place at Bogaziçi University, Istanbul, in 1999. The conference, *Redefinition of National Identity in the Age of Culturalist Politics*, was organized jointly by Günter Seufert, then irector of the Istanbul branch of the German Orient-Institut, and myself, and was funded by the Konrad Adenauer Foundation (Ankara), Körber Foundation (Hamburg), and Bogaziçi University Foundation (Istanbul). I am grateful to Günter Seufert for being the perfect friend and colleague, to Maurus Reinkowski and Karin Vorhoff for their contributions to the organization and eventual success of this exciting event, and to the funding organizations for making it possible.

Although there is some continuity between the conference and this book, as some of the present authors also participated in that event, the themes are different and none of the chapters in the present volume was actually presented at the conference. All chapters have been prepared for this collection, except Chapter 4 (by Soner Cagaptay) which is a modified version of an article originally published in the *Turkish Studies Association Bulletin* (vol. 25, no. 2/vol. 26, no. 1; Fall 2001/ Spring 2002). I thank the officers of the Turkish Studies Association for their permission to reprint this article.

Most of the editorial work on the book was done during a fellowship at the Woodrow Wilson International Center for Scholars (2002–3), which provided a most conducive environment for the pursuit of policy-oriented scholarship. I hope that this book will at least in some small measure repay my debt to the superb staff and scholars of the Wilson Center. I was also very fortunate to have Annika Kiessler, a brilliant young scholar, as my research assistant during the months that I worked on this book at the Center. Among other things, she is to be credited for her contribution to the translation of Riva Kastoryano's chapter from the French original.

I put the finishing touches to the manuscript while on a visiting scholarship at St Antony's College of the University of Oxford (February–April 2005), where the Middle East Centre and the South East European Studies Programme jointly offered a unique combination of warm friendship and stimulating intellectual environment.

My greatest debt is to Mark Selden, teacher and friend for his unwavering support for the publication of this project from beginning to end. He reviewed the material thoughtfully and offered incisive and constructive comments on each chapter. Most importantly, he gently but firmly challenged me, leading me to a major rethinking of the overall concept of the book.

Finally, I must acknowledge both the patience and the efficiency of the contributors, who met their deadlines despite the numerous unexpected setbacks along the way.

1 Introduction
Citizenship vs. nationality?

Haldun Gülalp

The modern nation-state is (ideally) a territorially circumscribed entity, exercising legitimate power within its boundaries. Citizenship in the modern state is (ideally) linked to territorial sovereignty, so that individual members of that community are accepted as equals regardless of their primary communal affiliations. But historical reality is much more complex than these normative principles. The nation-state is a specific and historically contingent model of political organization whose origins may be found in the Westphalian Treaty of 1648, signed at the end of the "Thirty Years" religious wars, which in effect started the era of mutual recognition of territorial sovereignties. As territorial powers began to acquire "national" legitimation, the "nation-state" form came into existence. The universality of this political form in the twentieth century has been the outcome of the imposition of the European model of territorial state on a global scale, both through colonization and other less direct modes of imposition (Poggi 1978, 1990; King 1986; Breuilly 1982; Hobsbawm 1992; Giddens 1995). Yet this outer shell of a common form of political organization, the nation-state, contains a bewildering variety of local experiences. Moreover, the variety in the patterns of citizenship is never solely limited to formal legislation and almost always has a popular cultural dimension. The formal principle by which the state defines citizenship is not necessarily the same as its actual practice. In many concrete cases, the formal structures of citizenship diverge from both the ideological claims of the nation-states and their actual policy-making practices. The study of the similarities and differences between the countries examined in this book reveals the universal dimensions of these issues.

Nation-states define their national communities in diverse ways, but the core elements of nationality usually include a combination of such historically rooted identities as religion, race, or ethnicity. Typically, an implicit or explicit ethnic or religious identity lies at the core of this definition and influences the state's treatment of its citizens. Thus, the modern state's building of the national community and its ongoing relationship with it necessarily involves a tension: the nation-state aims to tear individuals from their "traditional" (or "primordial") communal ties, and yet the conception of the nation still makes reference to a "traditional" identity. This essential tension, present from the inception of the nation-state, has been further deepened in recent years due to trends toward "globalization," which has weakened national boundaries and made them more porous. Both the re-emergence of already existing but heretofore suppressed minority identities and mass transnational migration have led to the creation of multiple sub-communities with distinct cultural identities within what presumably used to be coherent national communities.

The nation-state between ethnicity and globalization

The notion of citizenship is closely tied to the modern state's project of monopolizing the loyalties of individuals at the expense of their local, pre-national communities. In so far as citizenship implies the unification of a people around a state and the leveling of ranks by the creation of universal rights, it is identical to the building of a "nation" (Carr 1945; Marshall 1964). Citizenship therefore entails the creation of a new (national) community and a new (nationalist) ideology of political sovereignty. The concept of citizenship has two distinct aspects. First and foremost, it defines a new and politically constructed identity. As a system of closure, citizenship specifically identifies who is in, as a member of the national community, and who is out. Secondly, citizenship formally endows and burdens the members of the community with a set of rights and obligations. This is generally true regardless of the political regime of the nation-state. For example, in the same way that a liberal democratic nation-state grants the right of political participation only (or primarily) to its citizens, an illiberal and paternalistic nation-state that grants no or limited political rights but generous welfare benefits does so only (or primarily) to its own citizens. In both cases, state sovereignty is exercised in the name of the national community and is predicated upon nationalist ideology.

The greatest declared goal of nationalism, the dominant political ideology of the nineteenth and twentieth centuries, is the coincidence of nation and state; and the greatest myth of nation-states is that such coincidence is not only feasible but even nearly exists. Where there is an admitted divergence, "minorities" are created. This unavoidable situation raises a set of questions about sovereignty and to whom it really belongs. How will these divergent elements be made to fit into a supposedly homogeneous population that exercises sovereignty? Will the minorities be considered full members of that sovereign community? What will be their rights? How will those rights differ from, or converge with, the rights of the majority population, to which, it is assumed, real sovereignty belongs?

But even before the question of identifying what those differential rights or obligations may be, there is the question of how actually to define the minorities. There is no uniform concept that identifies minorities in all historical contexts. Minorities are not defined by a universally given set of criteria, but by a variety of them: linguistic, ethnic, racial, religious, sectarian, and so on. There is, in other words, a significant cultural dimension to the creation of minorities. One of the interesting dimensions of the history of nation-states is the "cultural construction" of the notion of citizenship, that is not only the official definitions provided by the state, but the popular-cultural concepts about who qualify and who do not qualify to become members of the community in the eyes of those who consider themselves to be the majority or the hegemonic (if not necessarily numerically dominant) element of that community.

In some cases, minorities are recognized as such from the inception of the nation-state, with the rest of the diverse elements of the population somehow brought into the (mythical) mold of a homogeneous nationality, while in others minorities are recent arrivals due to massive migration (whether drawn by job opportunities or propelled as refugees facing discrimination or annihilation). In yet some other cases, minorities have come into existence as a result of a group of citizens' assertion of their "cultural" difference and consequent demand for political recognition as such. These cases have proliferated in recent decades during which differential rights for minorities have begun to be perceived as a matter of universal human rights. Thus, while the pursuit of homogeneity through assimilation and the suppression of distinct identities was the norm in an earlier period of nationalism, today, in the age of globalization and culturalism, assertions of difference have become one of the primary vehicles of political struggle. In recent decades, the demand for "multiculturalism" has become a crucial concept in the popular contestation of the dominant definitions of citizenship.[1]

The language of culturalism and demand for "recognition" conceals the divergent sources of both the status and concerns of minorities. For instance, the Kurds in Turkey and the Turks in Germany may be treated as equivalent or at least comparable situations, although the former is a product of an old history of border drawing and nation building and the latter is a product of recent immigration. Attesting to the fluidity and variability of identities depending on the context, Kurdish-speaking immigrants from Turkey will still be called Turks in Germany. Nonetheless, the seeming similarity between these divergent cases reveals the myth of homogeneity; and the political language common to both has the cumulative effect of driving a wedge between political membership and cultural identity. Currently, the nation-state form of political sovereignty is under assault both from above and outside and from below and within. While globalization weakens and transforms the policy-making power of individual nation-states, the rising significance and urgency of cultural claims challenge the previously established forms of identity such as nation and class. This situation forces individual states to reassess and revise the established notions of citizenship, which have been formally defined by reference to a national community and granted by the nation-state as a set of social and political rights. Both globalization and culturalist movements complicate the imaginary coherence of national communities, question the existing terms of citizenship, and propose new foundations for political entitlement. Citizenship, as a system of closure that is based on nationality and contained within the boundaries of the nation-state, has begun to be revised and relaxed in the context of globalization, although not yet universally, as we shall see in the chapters below.

One alternative that has been emerging in recent years is the increase in multiple citizenships while another finds expression in the growth of the language of "human rights" and points at the need for institutions of supranational political community and democracy. In both cases, there is the increasingly pressing need to decouple rights from nationality (Soysal, Y. N. 1994; Faist 2004). Globalization seems to have opened up a postnational age of citizenship. While in the modern age of nationalism the normative expectation, however unrealistic, was for every nationality to aim to have its own independent state (Gellner 1983), in the postmodern age of globalization this is no longer the case. Nationality and political membership are now being separated. This is in stark contrast to an earlier era when the conflation between nationality and citizenship could be observed in both the interchangeable use of these two terms (which still continues to a certain extent) and the international legal norms that restricted multiple citizenships, such as the "Hague Convention" (1930), which stated that persons are entitled to only one nationality, and the "European Convention on Reduction of Cases of Multiple Nationality and Military Obligations in Cases of

Multiple Nationality" (1963), which has now been replaced by the much more liberal "European Convention on Nationality" (1997).[2]

As the rise of self-consciously "multicultural" societies ruptures the link between nationality and citizenship, territory and governance are likewise separated through the creation of supranational institutions that limit the sovereignty of individual nation-states, such as, most prominently, the European Union (EU), which arguably has gone well beyond earlier forms of supranational political communities. In fact, as soon as the formally independent nation-state became the universal norm in the second half of the twentieth century, supranational institutions began to emerge that to a certain extent appropriated the sovereignty of individual nation-states. These institutions currently include, in addition to the regulatory agencies of the global economy, such as the IMF and the World Bank, the whole gamut of multinational political and legal organizations from the UN to NATO, and multinational treaties from the European Covenant of Human Rights to the Kyoto Protocol (Held 1991, 2000; Slaughter 2003). But, as far as political representation at the global level is concerned, nation-states are still the relevant units for the negotiation of transnational issues. Despite the growing multiplicity and complexity of the institutions of global governance, the political actors that engage in these treaties and organizations are still the formally sovereign nation-states. While, for example, legitimation of political power is more and more based on the transnational concept of human rights, these rights are still granted and regulated by individual nation-states. Thus, individual citizens may have begun to seek their human rights in the global arena, often in the form of demanding protection from their own sovereign states, but they can do so only in so far as their nation-states have signed on to the requisite covenants.

The EU, however, is a novel political organization that aims to transcend the nation-state form. While on the one hand it has put into practice a regime of human rights on a supranational level, thereby separating citizenship rights from nationality, on the other hand it is an experiment in cosmopolitan democracy that was originally envisaged by some enlightenment philosophers. Both are trends anticipated and advocated by recent scholarship on citizenship (see, for example, Turner 1993, Archibugi and Held 1995, Bohman and Lutz-Bachman 1997, Linklater 1998, Vandenburg 2000, Ignatieff 2001, Falk and Strauss 2001). Still based on the assumptions of the Westphalian order, the UN, for example, takes the nation-states that comprise it as the relevant units of representation and does not discriminate between them for membership, which only requires formally independent state sovereignty and is not contingent on the character of the political regime. Dictatorships and liberal democracies sit side by side to negotiate global affairs as formally equal members in the UN. The Security Council rests on an entirely different power structure within the UN, but it too ignores the political regime of a member country. The EU, by contrast, is an association of liberal democracies. Moreover, as far as nation-state sovereignty is concerned, the EU and the UN appear to be based on opposing principles. While in order to qualify for UN membership a nation-state has to be recognized as fully sovereign, to qualify for EU membership a nation-state has to agree to surrender a significant measure of its sovereignty.

Comparative perspectives

The comparison of the countries studied in this book hinges on the way in which the state defines citizenship and determines who is or is not its citizen; it also addresses the impact of association with the EU on the transformation of these definitions. Each of these cases faces the perennial problem of building a nation-state: how to define the relationship between the nation-state and the ethnicity, religion, or any other communal identity of the population, and how to make that definition acceptable to the people who are in an actual or potential relationship of citizenship with that nation-state. The cases covered in this book represent a range of different modes of citizenship, and yet they all face similar problems. Despite their differences, as detailed below, in each of these countries some implicit or explicit ethnic or religious identity lies at the core of the national community and determines the state's definition and treatment of its citizens. In some cases, the existing notions of citizenship are being challenged by groups of people who feel that their political, economic, and social participation is hindered due to their religious or ethnic identities and hence express themselves through culturalist political mobilization with the aim to gain differential rights. In others, there is an effort to remove that ethnic or religious core from the definition of citizenship, with varying degrees of success. A comparison of these disparate cases shows that this common ambiguity in the construction of the nation (universalism vs. exclusionary communitarianism) is handled in different ways with differing outcomes, ranging from civil war to the peaceful redefinition of citizenship rights.

The six nation-states examined in this book have intertwined histories as well as revealing features of both convergence and divergence, as we see below. There are interesting links between them, both historical and ongoing. The most obvious is that many of these countries are descendants of the Ottoman Empire and products of the redrawing of the Middle Eastern map in the wake of wars. This is an important point to remember as, at the time of writing, the Middle East seems to be at yet another war-related crossroads in which borders are likely to be redrawn with serious consequences for citizenship and ethnic conflict.

The two, out of six, that do not descend from the Ottoman Empire are Germany and Israel; and they too have histories that are inextricably linked with each other, particularly through the horrors of the Nazi era, as well as with the other four, either as their neighbor (Israel) or as a receiver of Turkish immigrants and prominent actor in Turkey's prospective membership in the EU (Germany). There is also something in common between Germany and Israel, which is not exactly shared by the others, at least not in the same formal way: the claim to an exclusive ethnic identity as the basis of the nation-state, based on a line of descent through blood ties in the case of Germany and on religion in the case of Israel.

For the four states that do descend from the Ottoman Empire, however, the empire's *millet* system has been a powerful influence. Religion, rather than ethnicity or language, was the main basis of identification for the diverse subject populations of the Ottoman Empire; and the empire granted the various religious communities under its rule some form of autonomy in their internal affairs. A *millet*, then, was a religious community, which could include members of different ethnic and linguistic groups and residents of different regions of the empire, and which had some political power and significance. Each *millet* had its own semi-autonomous legal, judicial, as well as cultural and educational, functions, and was represented by a leader whose position was incorporated into the central administration of the empire. In the course of the nineteenth-century modernization of the Ottoman Empire, the term *millet* began to acquire its current meaning in the Turkish language, which is equivalent to the word "nation."[3]

But the Ottoman legacy has not been the only influence contributing to these four countries' nation-state formation experiences. Two of these four, Lebanon and Iraq, have also been colonized by "modern" colonial powers, France and Britain respectively, while the other two, Turkey and Greece, have never been colonized. The core remnant of the empire, that is Turkey, self-consciously rejected the Ottoman past and aimed to borrow from the French model of citizenship. The outcome was ambiguous, as we see below. Greece, on the other hand, whose nationalism was in many ways built, and to this day reproduced, in a dialectical relationship with Turkish nationalism, also claims, internally contradictorily, both Hellenic and Orthodox Christian sources of identity.

Finally, the state structures in both Iraq and Lebanon are powerfully shaped by their respective colonial experiences, most evidently in the fact that when Iraq gained independence from Britain it had the form of a monarchy, whereas France bequeathed its republicanism to independent Lebanon. Both, however, as colonies carved out of the Ottoman Empire, had borders drawn at negotiation tables between superpowers; and both have been, in effect, patchworks and seemingly interminable nation-building projects in progress.

Or, at least, that is how they are currently perceived. It is tempting, in other words, to think of these two examples as broadly representative of Middle Eastern (or, more generally, postcolonial) states, where nation-building has failed. The comparative framework of this book, however, suggests that the problem is more general and therefore its source lies elsewhere. If ethnic diversity challenges even those nation-states of the European core, where the myth of homogeneity has had a longer time to establish itself, and even if it does so for no other reason than the massive immigration of recent decades, then the problem perhaps lies in the assumptions of the nation-state form itself. Discarding the myth (and thus the presumed requirement) of homogeneity and liberating citizenship from nationality may be the only meaningful ways forward.

Diversity within unity

Germany is often presented as the archetype of the citizenship model that is based on the principle of ethnic descent (*jus sanguinis*), contrasted to the territorial principle (*jus soli*) epitomized by France (Brubaker 1992). In a piece that sets the tone for the general theoretical argument of the book, Riva Kastoryano (Chapter 2) examines the recent relaxation of the ethnicity-based, exclusionary citizenship law in Germany, where the sizable number of Turkish immigrants feel discriminated against. Kastoryano argues that the country's new citizenship law (2000), however revolutionary it may be for ending the "right of blood" principle (*jus sanguinis*), is not likely to integrate the Turks into German society, for government policy still constructs Turks as a homogeneous ethnic minority, despite their multiple internal divisions. Turks, in response, have demanded the right to "dual citizenship," which the new law does not recognize (although, admittedly, the restrictions of the law are not uniformly enforced throughout the country). The German government's denial of dual citizenship does not necessarily contribute to its presumed aim, that is the cultural assimilation of the Turks. On the contrary, focusing on the question of dual nationality perpetuates the distinction between true and false citizens. But this chapter also argues that, although demanded by the Turkish denizens of Germany as a democratic right, dual citizenship would still mark the bearer as less than a full citizen. Moreover, there is really nothing that is inherently democratic in the logic of dual citizenship, since citizenship can only be practiced within one territorial–political framework at a time.

The exclusionary character of German national identity has been at least partly responsible for the genocide against the Jews. Israel owes its legitimacy, if not its existence, to this horrific experience, and yet Israel itself is based on an exclusive religious identity. In fact, Israel well illustrates the inherent tension within the nation-state form, alluded to earlier. Zionism is on the one hand a modern ideology, influenced by the nationalist and socialist currents of nineteenth-century Europe, while on the other hand its legitimation is based on a dialog with the Old Testament. Moreover, it is precisely this exclusiveness in the definition of the nation (a quality desired in the ideology of all nation-states but never actually realized in history, despite attempts at the removal of the unwanted minorities) that belies the "democratic" assertions of the state of Israel. A critical review of the founding principles of Israel, as offered by Alain Dieckhoff (Chapter 5), reveals the tension between the secular and the religious elements among those principles. The analysis in this chapter demonstrates that the best way to understand the nature of the Israeli state is not to look at the plight of the Palestinians under occupation, although that has understandably been the primary concern of world public opinion, but at the Arabs who are citizens of Israel. An examination of the status of the Arab minority leads to the conclusion that, while Israel may be a democracy, it is also an ethnic state: hence an "ethnic democracy." The chapter proposes the recognition of collective rights for the Arabs, through a model of "consociational democracy," in order to overcome the ethnic bias of Israel's currently existing democracy and politically to integrate its Arab citizens on an equal footing.

Israel is not the only example where religion plays a key role in the definition of the nation. This is quite a common pattern, despite the obfuscation created by modernization theories that associate religion with tradition and the nation (and nationalism) with modernity.[4] Although the religious origin of national identity may be concealed in many cases, in some it is explicitly stated. The preamble to the Greek

Constitution declares that it is proclaimed "In the name of the Holy and Consubstantial and Indivisible Trinity" and Article 3 states that "The prevailing religion in Greece is that of the Eastern Orthodox Church of Christ." But, on the other hand, this appears in a tension with the Hellenic origin of Greek identity, retained through language. Like other nineteenth-century nationalisms, including Zionism, the ideologs of Greek nationalism were inspired by liberal, enlightenment ideas and, moreover, had the unique position of being able to claim a direct lineage to pre-Christian antiquity. For Greek nationalist intellectuals, as well as for European enlightenment philosophers, Greece was the source and direct ancestor of Europe. But, although this idea has remained both in competition and in an ambiguous alliance with the other source of Greek identity, defined through the Byzantine tradition and Orthodox Christianity, it is possible to say that the latter has eventually absorbed the former (Herzfeld 1986; Sherrard 1959). Effie Fokas (Chapter 3) explains this situation in terms of the legacy of the Ottoman *millet* system. In a comprehensive survey, Fokas details the historical periods in which both the significance of Orthodoxy as the core of Greek national identity and the consequent powerful role of the Orthodox Church in the political affairs of Greece have developed. Fokas also addresses the ways in which membership in the EU has begun to challenge the centrality of religion in Greece, generating resistance from the church hierarchy.

In Turkey, the place of religion in the definition of national identity is more concealed (and, perhaps, confused) than in Greece; but it is no less central. This should not come as a surprise, considering the fact that Greek and Turkish nationalisms were in part defined as a negation (and mutual exclusion) of each other. Modern Greek nationalism was constituted in a struggle of independence from the Ottoman Empire in the 1820s, and the Turkish nationalists won their decisive victory against the Greek armies in the 1920s. Yet, in some ways similarly to the ironic parallel between the German and Israeli exclusiveness, the mutual negation between Greece and Turkey had something in common at its core, which was best revealed in the exchange of populations between the two countries that took place in the aftermath of the creation of the new Turkish nation-state in 1923. In a mutual policy of national homogenizations between the Greek and Turkish governments, (Greek) Orthodox people living in Anatolia (Asian Turkey), even if they spoke Turkish as first language, were resettled in Greece; and, in exchange, Muslims living in mainland Greece (except Western Thrace) and on the islands, even if they spoke Greek as first language, were resettled in Turkey. This was only part of a more general pattern, whereby the Turkish nation was indeed created by the expulsion of the non-Muslim elements from the territory defined as Turkey (Hirschon 2003; Keyder 1987; Ahmad 1993). The remaining small populations of non-Muslims were given "minority" status and brought under protection (and granted some small measure of autonomy) by the Lausanne Treaty of 1923, the founding document of the Turkish Republic. Minority and non-Muslim are therefore identical in Turkish national consciousness.

This religious core of Turkish national identity seems to defy both the secularism (*laicité*) of the state and its territorial principle of citizenship, both enshrined in the Constitution and both borrowed from the French model. Established historiography uncritically portrays the Turkish state along these formal lines.[5] Recent scholarship, however, has shown that, in both popular cultural assumptions and state policy, the Turkish nation is primarily defined as a (Sunni) Muslim entity.[6] Through meticulous research into the immigration and citizenship policies of the state in the 1930s, the formative years of Turkish nationalism, Soner Cagaptay (Chapter 4) not only demonstrates the centrality of religion in Turkish identity, as a legacy of the Ottoman *millet* system, but also reveals the other layers added on to it. "Race" features among these layers, and comes to occupy an even more central place than religion; but, unlike the German conception of blood ties, here it is linked to language and culture. Finally, territory does indeed feature as an element of citizenship, but only as the remotest one of a number of concentric zones of Turkishness. Accordingly, Kurds, for example, as non-Turkish speaking Muslims, appear "assimilable" into the Turkish nation, while non-Muslims are seen as "inassimilable," even if they are citizens on the basis of the territorial principle.

A variant of the Ottoman *millet* system was actually retained in Lebanon, a province of the Ottoman Empire that became a French colony at the end of World War I. Lebanon's political system recognizes distinct religious "confessional" groups as political units endowed with rights. Thus, it replicates the *millet* system on a miniature scale, and is in fact much more generous than the Ottoman Empire had been in terms of the number of confessional groups that the state formally recognizes. At present, there are 18 such groups in Lebanon. The confessional system, which formally recognizes communal political rights (or, more precisely, the political powers of the communal leaders) by "distributing public offices, parliamentary seats, and ministerial portfolios proportionally among the country's main sects," coexists in a tension with a parliamentary system, complete with political parties and elections (Scheffler 2002).

While the chapter on Israel puts forward an argument in favor of a consociational model between the Jews and the Arabs, the discussion of the Lebanese "confessional system" by Maurus Reinkowski and Sofia Saadeh (Chapter 6) shows that this model of state, far from being a panacea, may actually deepen ethnic divisions and may even have contributed to the civil war in Lebanon. Hailed in the early post-World War II period as a rare democracy in the region up until its civil war, Lebanon at present still suffers from its "confessional" model of political organization and continues to experience the dead weight of religious leadership. This becomes especially clear in the critical review of the positions taken up by the different political blocs (i.e. confessional groups) of Lebanon, regarding the recent proposal for instituting "civil marriage" that transcends religious rules and divisions. An account of these debates, as offered in Chapter 6, demonstrates that confessionalism fails to recognize the political rights of individuals, qua individuals, and tends to empower only the heads of religious groups who wield their political power in favor of the status quo, which in turn seems to generate established interests among the population, contributing to the system's perpetuation.[7]

Iraq is often cited as another example of a divided society, similar to Lebanon, with the major difference that the three main sectors of society are not uniformly defined along religious lines, but rather on the basis of an incongruous combination of religion and linguistic ethnicity. Received wisdom on Iraq that speaks of "Kurds in the north, Sunnis in the center, and Shi'is in the south" conceals the fact that Kurds are also mostly Sunni, and that both the "Sunnis in the center" and the "Shi'is in the south" are also Arabs. As things stand, the Iraqi example seems perfectly to illustrate the tensions inherent in the general model of the nation-state itself: the nation is ideally imagined as a secular and unified entity, where individuals are torn from their communal identities and directly attached to the state, yet the nation-state also strives for "homogeneity" that is conceived in ethnic or religious (i.e. communal) terms. In this sense, Iraq remains to this day not only an unfinished, but even a seemingly impossible, project. Sami Zubaida (Chapter 7) argues, however, that the mentioned ethnic identities did not carry much significance in the age of nationalism, but were brought to the fore as a result of the patronage policies of the Ba'thist regime. This chapter's account of Iraqi nationalism also draws our attention to the marginalized status of the Jews in the Arab countries before the creation of the state of Israel and the outright hostility against them thereafter. The chapter thus describes the rise and decline of Iraqi nationalism, and the ultimate fragmentation by the Ba'thist regime of the entity originally imagined as a unified nation.

In this instance, as in others, what are known as primordial affiliations are really historically constructed, albeit sociologically and politically significant, collectivities. Thus it appears that those associations that rely on "primordial" sources of identity are formed either in the absence of political alternatives or as a result of political manipulations by the dominant elite. Moreover, they are not due to any "exotic" character of non-Western societies, where, it is often believed, primordial divisions make modern democracy unviable. Historians may still debate how much of the regime of "confessionalism" in Lebanon is really due to the Ottoman legacy and how much of it is due to the expediencies of French colonialism. They may likewise debate how much this regime is to be blamed for the recent civil war and the continuing political instability in Lebanon. But how can Iraq's and Lebanon's political difficulties be understood without considering the policies of neighboring Israel or Western interests in the oil resources of the region? The Lebanese and Iraqi experiences may provide us with an important lesson in the context of yet another war in the region, where the proposed new regime in Iraq sounds alarmingly similar to the one already in existence in Lebanon. Likewise, the proposed possibility of carving an independent Kurdish state out of Iraq sounds alarmingly similar to the pure ethnic model of state currently (and thankfully) being left behind in Germany. Clearly, if either one of these proposals comes to pass, it will not be possible to blame it on the atavistic tendencies presumed to be inherent in Middle Eastern peoples. On the contrary, both of these projects originate in the power centers of the West and aspire to anachronistic models of state building.

Peaceful transition or implosion?

Each of the cases examined in this book illustrates both the ambiguity in the definition of the boundaries of the national community and the implicit or explicit significance attached to a "primordial" identity in the conception of the nation as a political community. But comparing these disparate cases also suggests an interesting pattern, which is reflected in the order in which the chapters are presented. The first three countries examined here, Germany, Greece, and Turkey, despite their different historical trajectories, appear to have converged along the same path of transforming their citizenship laws, practices and/or cultural perceptions in favor of greater pluralism and liberalism in the context of their association with the EU.[8] The other three, however, seem to be in a permanent state of crisis, in which deepening ethnic conflicts appear to make peace nearly impossible.

We have already noted the irony in the similarity of the German and Israeli notions of citizenship. In both Germany and Israel, citizenship has been dominated by an exclusionary principle of ethnicity, and both countries have had large populations who have been permanent residents within their borders but effectively denied full rights of citizenship. This is where the similarity ends, however, for Germany, in the process of European unification, and as a leading power within that Union, has come to accept the shortcomings of its nationality principle and recently taken steps to revise it politically and legally. Israel, by contrast, has moved in the opposite direction during that same period, acting to deprive non-Jews, both citizens and others, of basic human and civic rights. Likewise, as we see in the chapters below, there is a striking similarity between Greece and Lebanon in terms of the way in which religious leaders intervene in political affairs and try to block reform. Yet equally striking is the fact that while in Lebanon they continue to be successful, in Greece they have ultimately failed. We find that in Greece the normative context of EU membership has significantly shifted the balance of forces.

What we see in Greece is replicated in Turkey. The Turkish government's treatment of minorities has improved dramatically in recent years, mostly thanks to reforms introduced under EU pressure (or, more precisely, with the prospect and promise of ultimate EU membership, through convictions by the European Court of Human Rights, and finally by the sheer pressure of the public sentiment that the nation needs to conform to global/European norms). Indeed, after the end of the military conflict between the Turkish state and Kurdish rebels that had consumed fifteen years and (by the government's oft-cited figure) 30,000 lives, the EU process acted like a magic wand, reversing the customary oppressive policies of Turkish governments. Also similarly to the Greek example, resistance to many EU-related reforms is expressed through protesting the loss not only of sovereignty but, more gravely, of historically rooted cultural identity. Conversely, though, these reforms have been driven forward against the conservative forces within the country by using the leverage of the EU institutions and the prospect of ultimate membership (Gülalp 2005). Thus, in Turkey, as in Greece, internal political reform has been a matter of "foreign affairs." The EU, as an institution, but also as an abstract concept defining a civilizational project, appears to have been directly inserted as a key player into the internal political process of these countries.

One may be led to believe that this "demonstration effect" (to borrow a term from economic theory) is more easily comprehensible in the case of Greece and Turkey, both of which lie on the margins of

Europe. "Cultural intimacy," in Michael Herzfeld's apt phrase, points to the shared knowledge in Greek consciousness that the role assigned to them by the West of being the origin and spiritual ancestor of European civilization conflicts with the reality of being (and feeling) an outsider (Herzfeld 1997, 2002). It is this gap between intimate knowledge about the self and the image that needs to be displayed that turns Europe (even as an abstract concept) into such a central player, as brilliantly described by Effie Fokas, below.[9] The gap may have a different shape in Turkey, but it does exist all the same. An important player in European power politics during the Ottoman period, but always left outside of the continent's "civilizational" framework because of Islam, Turks have equally been concerned with their ambivalent place in the world. Especially in the nineteenth-century modernization of Europe, when the Ottomans were in relative decline, a desperate struggle to prove to the Western world that they had the right to exist made the Ottomans sensitive to the European gaze and obsessed with their image (Deringil 1998: pp. 150–65). Turks continue to operate from a position of having internalized much of the unflattering Western view about themselves, accounting for the power of the "demonstration effect." But the same effect can also be observed in Germany, a core founder of the EU. With a past they want to distance themselves from, the political elites of Germany have wholeheartedly signed on to the project of European integration. This "politics of the European identity of Germany" has helped the political elites to defer domestic issues to supranational processes. Presenting a particular policy as being in line with European interests has been highly effective in silencing the opposition (Risse and Engelmann-Martin 2002).[10]

Here we find, then, in the first category of countries, Germany, a core country and one of the founders of the EU, together with Greece, simultaneously defined as the source of European civilization and a marginal member lying on the border of Europe, and Turkey, a predominantly Muslim nation that might only be admitted into full EU membership if deemed useful for European strategic interests in helping prevent the dreaded "clash of civilizations." Yet there is a similarity in the way in which these three disparate cases have transformed themselves. In the latter category, together with Israel, we find two Arab countries, Iraq and Lebanon, one predominantly Muslim and the other multi-confessional, both remnants of the Ottoman Empire but each subsequently colonized by a different rival European power.

This pattern defies all received modes of classification and cuts across worn-out dividing lines, such as Muslim vs. Christian, Jew vs. Gentile, Arab vs. non-Arab, and so on. However paradoxical it may seem given the significance attached to the abstract concept of "Europe" and its norms, this pattern does not even fit the more innocuous European vs. Middle Eastern divide. This is not only because of the many characteristics that both Turkey and Greece share, due to their common Ottoman heritage (the mother of all Middle Eastern identities) with Lebanon and Iraq, but also because of the fact that the EU project is an outcome not only of the achievements of Europe but also of its failures. We would do well to remember that the common history of European nations that now make up the EU is one of bloody wars along dividing lines of race and religion, as well as ideology and imperialistic ambition. It is this that accounts for the joint need to create a zone of peace such as the EU. As Luisa Passerini (2002: p. 195) reminds us, we should avoid "attaching the notion of European identity to the idea (and the reality) of a united Europe." She adds, "A similar distance must be maintained between the historical forms of European identity and forms that are possible for the future." In other words, in the same way that we ought to remove nationality from citizenship within the political community, we must also remove an essentialist or culturalist concept of European identity from the political project of the EU. European identity within the EU is as much a myth as nationality within the nation-state. Finally, the comparisons between these two groups of countries confirm a point that should not even have been necessary to reiterate: democratic reform by "invitation" is far more preferable to, and certainly much more effective than, regime change by "invasion."

As far as the three countries in the latter category are concerned, we are unable to predict in any meaningful way, at the time of writing, how events in Iraq and Israel will unfold. There is no doubt, of course, that the political future of Lebanon, as well as other countries in the region (and beyond), will depend to a large extent on the outcome of the ongoing conflicts both in Iraq and between Israel and the Palestinians. Peace within Lebanon has been maintained so far through the acrobatic maneuvers of political actors who have to negotiate a formally democratic parliamentary regime encumbered with the reality of the confessional system, but it seems precarious indeed. *Solidere*, and its ambitious project of reviving the central district of Beirut, may have been an important part of the answer to the question of what has maintained peace in the post-civil war era in Lebanon.[11] The warlords have entered the civilian government as partners in the pie that is growing with the flow of money coming in for this reconstruction and the economic boom that is expected to follow from it. Anyone who visits downtown Beirut will doubtless be fascinated by the amount of money and effort poured into real estate development in the central district and its striking contrast with the poor neighborhoods only within walking distance. The economic pie that is shared between the elites of the confessional groups may be trickling down to a certain extent, incorporating the popular base of these leaders into the bonanza, which, however, has also cost Lebanon a foreign debt of over $30 billion.

But there is an additional and highly dangerous complication. Lebanon is "protected" (in official parlance) by Syria and shares borders with Israel. The border with Israel is defended by fighters, who are also represented in the Lebanese parliament by their political wing, but are listed by both Israel and the USA as a terrorist organization, with links to both Syria and Iran. It is almost that, as if the Lebanese hybrid system of combining parliamentary democracy with confessional power-sharing is not difficult enough to cope with, maintaining the peace also requires navigating the stormy waters of the politics of war and imperialism in the region, sometimes leading to what might appear as confusing outcomes such as the cooperation of the Sunni Muslims in Lebanon with the USA and of the Maronite Christians with Syria. The shocking news, received as these lines were being written, of the assassination of Rafik Hariri, who had been the driving force of the economic reconstruction of Beirut, both as a wealthy businessman who founded *Solidere* and as the Lebanese Prime Minister for most of the post-civil war period, does not augur well for the future. Out of the country during the civil war, he had no direct ties to the warlords, but had made himself indispensable in the post-war period: until, in the fall of 2004, international pressure began to mount on Syria to withdraw its forces from Lebanon, to which Syria responded by dragging its feet, and Hariri resigned his post as Prime Minister, appearing to side with the anti-Syrian forces. Under these circumstances, it is impossible not to fear for the renewal of the nightmare of 1975–90.

Notes

1 There is a huge literature that documents and examines this. For some of the most representative examples, see Gutmann (1994, 2003), Phillips (1995, 1999), Wilmsen and McAllister (1996), Benhabib (1996, 2002), Barry (2001).
2 See Faist (2004). There is no doubt that "security" concerns have been paramount in these efforts to restrict multiple citizenships (as was the case when the widespread institution of passports began with the outbreak of World War I, after a long period of "liberal" immigration policies in the latter half of the nineteenth century). (Torpey 2001).
3 On the Ottoman *millet* system, see Karpat (1973, 1982).
4 As, for example, is the case in Britain, India, Japan, and the Netherlands, among others. See Van der Veer and Lehmann (1999).

5 For instance, according to Enver Ziya Karal (1981: p. 18), "Turkey is a geographical concept: the Turkish people are those who inhabit Anatolia and Thrace." He adds, "This definition by Atatürk reflects a nineteenth-century view of nationhood."

6 See Yegen (2004). One might also question the reality of the formal conception of territorial citizenship in France itself, where, according to Eric Hobsbawm (1977: p. 241), during the rule of Napoleon III, citizenship was opened to native Algerians on the condition that they give up belief in Islam: a pattern that appears to be repeated in the recent ban on wearing "conspicuous religious symbols" in public schools, notably the Muslim women's headscarves. See Balibar (2004, especially fn. 4), where he borrows Edgar Morin's phrase "*catholaicité*" to describe the regime under which "France has in fact lived for two centuries."

7 As Anne Phillips (1995: p. 16) points out, "The most favorable conditions for a stable consociational democracy are those in which the spokespeople for each segment have relatively unchallenged authority.…." An implication of this observation is that the civil war may have been caused by a challenge from below to the segmentary hierarchy of the Lebanese confessional system. Based on this, one might further argue that in both Lebanon and Israel the common problem seems to be the confessional framework of nationhood. In both cases, therefore, it seems that deconfessionalization would be the key to the elimination of political tensions and the realization of peace.

8 For a detailed examination of the evolution of EU policies and legislation on the rights of minorities, see Bruno de Witte (2001).

9 See, also, Dia Anagnostou (2001) for a discussion of how the framework of the EU and the language of European norms contributed to easing the tensions between the Christian majority and the Muslim minority in Greece.

10 See, also, Peter Katzenstein (1997) for the "Europeanization of Germany."

11 *Solidere*, as described in its own propaganda literature, is "a joint stock corporation established in May 1994 through an association of former property rights holders in the Beirut Central District and investors who responded to an IPO of $650 million. The total capital stands at $1.65 billion in real estate and cash, with shareholders numbering about 100,000."

2 Redefining German unity

From nationality to citizenship

Riva Kastoryano

Since 1 January 2000, a child born in Germany to foreign parents acquires German citizenship if one of the parents has lawfully resided in Germany for at least eight consecutive years.[1] The new law thus marks a historical turning point by replacing the right of blood and affiliation (*jus sanguinis*), in force since 1913, by the right of soil (*jus soli*). Its adoption by the *Bundesrat* in May 1999 was the result of long negotiations between political parties on one side, and the federal government and immigrants on the other. All political parties agree upon the need to integrate foreigners who have been living in German territory into the national community, while the immigrants themselves would only accept German citizenship along with the right to keep their original nationality. The question is how to combine ideology and reality, rhetoric, and law in a way that underlines a compromise between political morality and juridical limits?

The question of citizenship in Germany came to the fore in the German public debate with the massive arrival of the *Aussiedler* (immigrants of German descent) after the fall of the Berlin Wall and the collapse of the Soviet Union. Indeed, these people from central Europe and Russia were naturalized de facto and on oath by simple proof of their affiliation and their belonging to the German "people," whereas other foreign people, who have been settled in Germany for more than 30 years and socialized within its local and national institutions, still remain excluded from the political community for reasons of ancestry (i.e. the fundamental principle of *jus sanguinis*). The discretionary naturalization of immigrants therefore raises the question of political ethics that has fueled the debate on the citizenship rights of "foreigners by blood." Focusing on the prospect of dual citizenship, which is prohibited by the Constitution but claimed by the Turks as a condition of access to equal citizenship, the debate became rather emotional in the ranks of both the opposition and public opinion, leading Schröder, who had originally included it in his bill, eventually to remove this clause.

The idea of dual citizenship implies a distinction between citizenship and nationality: two interdependent and "interchangeable"(Leca 1992: pp. 13–50) concepts within the framework of the nation-state, which determine the affiliation of the individual to a political community. This affiliation is realized through the rights (social, political, and cultural) and duties inherent to the idea of citizenship. But affiliation to a community is not limited to the law. The juridical act that affirms this principle supports the integration of "foreigners" into the national community on the condition that they share the same moral and political values. The foreigner is expected to be familiar with, and to adhere to, the state's historical references as a proof of loyalty to the fundamental principles of the nation (which, according to Weber, constitutes the only community that emerged from modernity).

These are, at least, the expectations. They are based on the founding principles of the nation-state, on its political traditions, and more precisely on what has become its national identity. This is as true for Germany as for France: two republics marked by different histories and portrayed as two systematically opposed ideal–typical "models" of citizenship and nationality. According to these models, France represents the prime example of a nation-state, which conceives of itself as "universalist" for being assimilationist and egalitarian, whereas Germany is an exclusivist nation that privileges common ancestry and belonging to the same cultural community. These differences serve as a rhetorical basis to the debate, to animate public opinion and shape modes of thought. At the same time, they affect institutional practices and determine the juridical principles for access to citizenship: France privileges socialization within French territory and by its institutions, whereas Germany maintained until recently laws that exclusively rely on the cult of "ancestors" (Brubaker 1992; Dumont 1991).

But social realities bring the two countries closer together in terms of both discourse and law.[2] As a matter of fact, German citizenship cannot be considered separately from its political conception, and, by the same token, French citizenship cannot be abstracted from the element of cultural identification and transmission. With regard to community organization by the immigrant populations and their claim for the recognition of one or more cultural particularities, both nations express a similar feeling of "suspicion" towards the immigrant: a sentiment that comes up in any debate on immigration and citizenship and that undeniably reveals the political elite's and the public's apprehension of seeing nationality "desacralized" by a "citizenship on (and for) paper," that is a right without identity. Arguments that inflame public debate often refer to the attachment, whether real or imaginary, of the "immigrants" or the "foreigners" to their home country, which is perceived as a distinct identification with a national or religious community that resides within the political community. While in France it is the political rhetoric (by means of ignorance) that rejects all political affiliation to a community other than the national one, in Germany it is the Constitution that requires all naturalized citizens to renounce their nationality of origin as a proof of "complete" adherence to German nationality. This largely explains the controversies of the debate on dual citizenship that agitated passions and emotions ever since the bill was prepared and eventually submitted to the parliament in January 1999.

The debate on citizenship refers to rights and identities, to moral and political values, and to the sharing of civic responsibilities within a given political community (see Pickus 1998). As a result, it has led to negotiations of identity between the states and their immigrants (Kastoryano 2002). From the states' point of view, the question is how to negotiate new modes of integration for immigrant people into the political community, on the basis of a new balance between evolving community structures and national institutions. Based on the principle of equality, the primary concern for individuals or groups is to fight against any form of exclusion, be it political, social, or cultural, and to show attachment to both the national community and a collective identity other than the national one. This inevitably challenges the traditionally established link between cultural community and political belonging, that is between nation and state, between nationality and citizenship: the former as a source of identity and the latter as a right to civic participation with equal rights. It is this tendency that has been a source of today's rhetorical and juridical changes in democratic states: a citizenship with multiple references of identity, even with the same civic responsibility towards the political community, leading to the replacement of the "dream of cultural unity" by a "dream of political unity."

The dream of German unity

The dream of national unity is strongly linked to German Romanticism. In his "Address to the German nation," Fichte insisted on the idea of the cultural unity of the German nation. Elements like cultural unity and the unity of language (advocated by Herder) have nurtured the German dream of national unity. They have circumscribed a collective identity for all those who shared the same ancestors, the same language, and the same culture. The German nationalism inspired by Fichte has at the same time been the product of a resistance to foreign "domination," accompanied by élans and passions. "Unity, justice and freedom" (*Einigkeit und Recht und Freiheit*) become the determining values of the German nation. They first appeared in the "Song of the Germans" (*Deutschlandlied*) written by August Heinrich Hoffmann von Fallersleben and were later incorporated into the national anthem of the Federal Republic in 1952.

German Romanticism emerged at the beginning of the nineteenth century as a reaction to France and its revolutionary ideas, leading Germany to a "communitarian" reply. Indeed, German Romanticism, by privileging the feeling of belonging to a culture or a people, collides with the rationality that had inspired the Revolution and opposes its universal values. In contrast to the religious rationale that characterizes the Age of Enlightenment (and which Fichte characterizes as the reason for the Prussian defeat), Romanticism re-evaluates the religious element of social cohesion. While Prussian reformers who were inspired by the French Revolution conceived the initial plans for a constitutional state, the Romantics nostalgically referred to Christianity unifying the people of Europe in the Middle Ages: "the only epoch in German history where the nation knew a brilliant and glorious existence, with a rank befitting a people with deep roots."[3]

The difference with the Age of Enlightenment is expressed by the notion of *Volksgeist* (spirit of the people), which becomes the constitutive element of the German nation (Brubaker 1992: p. 9). Hence, this leads to the development of the idea of *Volksnation* (nation of the people). Such a conception of the German nation fuels fears of losing identity and, as it remains rooted in the past, it serves as a refuge: the Holy Roman Empire, the ancestors, and the feeling of belonging to a community of heritage. This community is "imagined" through organic links between individuals who share the same culture, and finds expression in the feeling of belonging to the German people, even though it is geographically dispersed in empires that have no communication with one another. The reference to the German people, *Das Deutsche Volk*, therefore emphasizes a belonging that is primarily ethnic. This concept does not allow any cultural difference: in fact, the cultural unity and the organic character of the national community are expressed by the very definition of the nation. As early as 1849, the idea of "Germanness" (*Deutschtum*), which also implied Germans living in neighboring states, animated the debate on the Constitution. In fact, the latter referred to nationality as a German particularity and to the fundamental rights of the "German people," who de facto were German citizens (see Gosewinkel 1998: pp. 125–35). Culture and politics are thus combined, so that a cultural identity constitutes the basis of a political identity.

The movement of nationalist ideas goes back to the revolutionary period and the unification of the German State in 1871. Thus, the idea of nation, which was cultural at first, has preceded the birth of the state, and the national conscience was elaborated earlier than any political structure. Therefore, the idea of nationality based upon blood-right already posed a conceptual and practical problem at the time of its formation, insofar as the new frontiers of the Empire brought the concepts of people and territory into conflict. Hence, the little Germany excluded foreigners coming from neighbouring states, but principally included ethnic Germans living outside of its borders. Moreover, the absence of a center, revealed in the weakness of political institutions, contributed not to the shaping of any form of political identification, but rather to a sense of ethnocultural belonging (*Volksgemeinschaft*) founded upon the principle of descent. As Roger Brubaker (1992) points out, this resulted in two forms of citizenship: a political one, corresponding to the territory, and a spiritual and ethnic one, founded upon common ancestors. Also, the "Nationality Law of the German Empire and States" adopted in 1913 and in effect until January 2000, upheld the ethnic dimension of citizenship, by allowing Germans living outside the borders to keep the German nationality (*Aussiedler*) and by denying the latter to foreigners born on German territory.

German identity, which consequently crossed the borders of the Empire, did not automatically have a recognized political meaning in the new state. Nevertheless, this did not prevent the two factors of ancestry and territory (of the past) to be combined under the definition of nationality, so that the Germans living outside the state's borders would keep at least their German nationality. In 1949, the Fundamental Law confirmed the principle of a citizenship which was linked to belonging to the German people. Article 116 of this law declares any individual of German descent and living within the borders of the Empire to be German.

Such a representation of the nation calls upon the law in the case of the *Aussiedler* (i.e. people of German descent who were living on the territory of the former Empire). Their naturalization by law upon proof of belonging to the German people at the moment of their arrival leads to a confrontation between territory (still of the past), culture, and identity. Culture and identity are dynamic concepts, which vary by time and through interactions. As a result, their usage in the present in direct reference to the past immediately creates an ambiguity regarding social reality, exposed, for instance, by the problematic cultural and social integration of the *Aussiedler*. Several studies have examined their difficulty of adaptation and degree of integration, as well as the way they are perceived by Western German society in social and cultural terms. Despite the assumption of having common ancestors, the *Aussiedler* appear more foreign to the German language and culture, and especially to its politics, than immigrants, who were often born on German territory or at least socialized within its national institutions. In sociological terms, they even seem to constitute a new social category, causing Germans living on the territory of the nation-state to call themselves *Einheimische* or even *Bundesdeutsche* ("Germans of stock"), in order to distinguish themselves from the Germans "from outside of the territory" (Dietz 1999: pp. 153–76).

Nation and immigration in Germany

Such a representation of the nation found an echo in the official discourse which until recently repeated that "Germany is not a country of immigration." Recently, however, several studies have begun to attest to the opposite: "Germany is a country of immigration" (see, for example, Münz, Seifer, and Ulrich 1997).

Germany's immigration is above all the result of an employment policy. At the end of the nineteenth century, industrialization, or rather the transition of "an agricultural State with a strong industry into an industrial State with an important agricultural base," had at first provoked an internal migration from the East to the West (Bade 1984, 1994: pp. 442–55). In most cases, those migrants were German Poles. But eventually, towards the end of the century, the number of foreign Poles from Russia and Austria had by far exceeded the number of German Poles working in the agricultural sector of the East. The ongoing immigration, which took place despite the labor shortage in Silesia and Russia, alarmed the German authorities. They became concerned about the "Polonization" of the West that might result from the contact between German Poles and non-German Poles working side by side. Seasonal work from then on appeared to be the best way to combine economic interests with protection against foreign "invasion" (*Überfremdung*). Thus, a rotation system emerged, which was enforced by controlling conformity to the limitations of the working period (*Karenzzeit*) for foreign Poles in the West. But, at the same time, the permanent need for cheap labor due to industrialization led to what has been called the recourse to "the industrial reserve army," formed by Dutch, Austrian, and especially Italian workers, which subsequently changed the structure of the foreign population. After World War II, foreign labor became crucial for economic reconstruction. This time, people came from the east of the Mediterranean, including Greece, former Yugoslavia, and Turkey.

At present, almost 7 million foreigners live in Germany, 2.5 million of whom have Turkish nationality. Their presence goes back to the 1960s: a presence that has until recently been "assimilated" to a temporary stay, giving a false idea about the reality of immigration and communicating hope through a discourse which encouraged return. Later, this kind of discourse actually paved the way for the so-called "Foreigner Politics" (*Ausländerpolitik*). In the 1980s, even a bill on citizenship was titled "laws for foreigners" (*Ausländergesetz*). Such a stand showed that there was no will to allow the *Ausländer* (the foreigners) to have more than a foreigner's status. They would have to remain at the margin of the nation and of citizenship. Their future as citizens or as a part of the national community would be ignored. From this perspective, naturalization could only be conceived as the ultimate stage of assimilation.

At the same time in the 1980s, both Germany and France defined themselves as "multicultural." The Frankfurt municipality even established a department of "multicultural affairs," headed by the Vice-Mayor of the city, Daniel Cohn-Bendit, who pleaded for a "multicultural democracy, inspired by Rousseau's social contract."[4] But the use of this term implies a strategy of representation and a statement about a society in which people of different nationalities and religions coexist. With regard to a democratic society, which is based on the principle of the equality of rights, this sort of discourse is aimed at encouraging public opinion to accept (anthropological) diversity as an inherent fact of any modern society. According to the active members and spokesmen of opposition parties, this can be seen as a way of helping the public and the political elite to realize that "foreigners are here to stay," and that Germany is a country of immigration and a de facto multicultural society. Hence, the *Gastarbeiter* (guest workers) became *Ausländer* (foreigners). In the 1970s, they were called *ausländische Arbeiter* (foreign workers) or sometimes *Einwanderer* (immigrants). Now they were not merely *Gäste* (guests) anymore, but immigrants or minorities, or both: *Einwanderungsminorität* (the immigrant minority) or even *ausländische Mitbürger* (foreign co-citizens): that is citizens without really being them.

The terminology, even with the changes, underlines the persistent perception about the foreigner. It shows once again the influence of mentality on institutional structures and the relation between rhetoric and jurisdiction: basic elements of the debate on citizenship. Indeed, the immigration in the 1960s, as much as at the beginning of the century, had been labeled the "the importation of workers" (see Bade 1984, 1994). Since that time, the foreign presence has not had any impact on the laws on "Germanness" and German nationality. The latter, although contested as an impediment to democratic principles, appeared coherent with the definition it provided for the German nation. If the German nation is defined by a common ethnicity, the basic principle of nationality remains linked to common ancestors and is founded on "blood" (*jus sanguinis*). But in 1993, a new law on foreigners (*Ausländergesetz*) was passed in reaction to the flux of immigration from the East, in order to facilitate their integration. The law seemed to express a "moral obligation" toward foreigners living on German soil for three generations. This law introduced for the first time a criterion for the socialization of the grandchildren of the *Gastarbeiter* who were candidates for naturalization. Accordingly, a young foreigner could obtain naturalization by law under the following conditions: he or she has to apply between the ages of 16 and 23, has to have been resident in the Federal Republic of Germany for eight unbroken years, has to have been attending an educational establishment for six years (at least four years of it in an establishment of general education), and finally has to have no criminal record. Moreover, the fee for naturalization that varied between DM3,000 and DM5,000 was reduced to DM100 for these young people. The number of naturalized foreigners, which represented between 20,000 and 30,000 people per year between 1973 and 1989, reached 101,377 in 1990. In 1993, more than 29,000 foreigners obtained German nationality by legalizing their undocumented immigrant status and 44,900 by naturalization upon the discretionary decisions of the German authorities.[5]

In 1994, the coalition government between the Christian Democrats and the Free Democrats came up with another initiative that concerned the third generation children of Turkish origin. In public debate this was referred to as "infant citizenship" (*Kindesstaatsangehörigkeit*). The objective of the bill in question was to grant German nationality at birth to a child with foreign parents, under the condition that one of the parents was also born in the Federal Republic. All in all, this introduced a "double *jus soli*" similar to that practiced in France, but it also required the married couple to provide a proof of residence in Germany for at least 10 years before the child's birth. At the age of 18, the child would be granted the opportunity to choose between German nationality and the parents' nationality. There was also the question of whether or not to give those children a "guarantee of naturalization"

(*Einbürgerungszusicherung*), which would be noted on their identity card at birth.[6] In this context, one should keep in mind that the German Constitution prescribes a single nationality, which means that in order to become German by law one has to renounce one's original nationality.

Participation and citizenship

Obviously, the laws that regulate citizenship affect the modes of participation as well as the strategies of the actors. The lack of political rights, which are only granted with the status of legal citizenship, leads foreigners to develop new strategies: strategies of compensation. This, however, does not exclude their integration; on the contrary, it encourages the foreigners to seek indirect ways of recognition. Thus, a citizen is no longer just a "spectator who votes," in Rousseau's words, but rather an actor who seeks to express his vote by influencing public opinion and government policy.

The demand for the recognition of identity-related cultural specifics has driven the "foreigners" to participate in the public sphere, a common space of socialization and exercise of power, and thereby to demonstrate their engagement and their de facto belonging to a political community. This engagement can be seen especially in their participation in associations that are recognized by the public authorities, but also in the activities of local communities (of cultural or ethnic nature) and in the economy: briefly, in civil society in general. This is how citizenship is practiced. It is a sort of citizenship that mainly derives from social practice. All in all, it constitutes the expression of the individual's commitment to the common good represented by the national community.[7]

In fact, the ever-increasing number of immigrant associations since the 1980s can be explained by the so-called "politics of foreigners" (*Ausländerpolitik*), which aims at their integration, as contradictory as this terminology might appear. The German government thus encourages foreigners to organize themselves (*Selbsthilfe*) in associations. The idea is to encourage them to create their own organizations to combat delinquency, poverty, and criminality. This practice is reminiscent of American liberalism where voluntary associations of ethnic communities provide mutual aid or charity services to their members, and moreover endeavor to administer their social problems. In Germany, these ethnic communities that are highly organized and that deliver all sorts of support to their members also engage in the struggle for equal rights as expressed by the very definition of citizenship. Such a community identifies itself in relation to civil society, where organizations and political actions take form. It actually appears as an extension of the corporatist system that characterizes the civil society of non-citizens: on the basis of residence, and aspiring to an equality of rights that would correspond to a sort of citizenship. Finally, this shows the Turks' aspiration to integrate into the social structure of the Federal Republic (along the lines of para-public or semi-sovereign institutions that belong to civil society and play an important role in political decision-making).[8]

On the local level, their engagement became more concrete with the establishment of structures such as the advisory boards for foreigners (*Ausländerbeiräte*), created in the middle of the 1970s, or the "extra-municipal commissions of foreigners."[9] These organizations enable the "non-nationals" (in the official terminology of the Federal Republic) to commit themselves to the "common good" – in this case, a particular town or city. Foreigners organized in such structures seek to represent common interests within the municipality and are most often concerned with schools, kindergartens, and public parks (*Grünflächen*) or commerce. The establishment of autonomous lists of candidates for these boards generates fierce competition, and occasionally causes inter-ethnic tensions in these cities as well as within or between the different associations.

However, the purely symbolic character of these advisory boards prevents their elected members from exercising any significant influence upon communal decision-making. In fact, their role is limited to submitting to the local authorities either proposals that deal with the problems of foreign businessmen and students or reports aimed at revealing the dysfunctions of immigration authorities. Nevertheless, their elections draw great attention. For example, in the election for the Advisory Board in Bamberg in the fall of 1994, the rate of foreigners' participation increased to 48.5 percent in general and to 78 percent among the Turks, whose candidates also won several seats (Yalçin-Heckmann 1995).

In addition to the impact of associations and local mobilization on public opinion, integration into civil society also takes place through economic success as evidence of citizenship (Walzer 1994). According to a report published in 1991 in Brussels, an estimated DM57 billion of direct or indirect income was brought in by Turks. This sum surpassed by far the DM16 billion spent on foreigners by the welfare state.[10] The associations of Turkish businessmen estimated in 1992 that 35,000 Turkish entrepreneurs, from the restaurateur to the industrialist, employed a total of 150,000 Turks and 75,000 Germans. Their annual income reached DM25 billion, and in 1991, they paid DM1 billion in taxes.[11] These economic actors do not only play an important role in the relations between Germany and Turkey, but they also exert a considerable influence on German investment projects in the Turkic republics of the former Soviet Union. The statistics regularly survey the state of their investments and the media draw attention to their consumption, while German enterprises express their civil solidarity and thereby seek to influence the policies that might concern them.

But can security based on economic presence compensate for the political insecurity which stems from a lack of juridical protection? Can economic integration open up the path to political rights? History provides a partial answer to this question. The economic environment of the nineteenth century forced Germany into international economic competition during the Great Depression of 1873 to 1896. This is how the economy eventually gained importance and began to influence the political decisions of the country. By the same logic, certain sectors of activity, such as the organization of Turkish doctors since 1990 and businessmen's associations from different *Länder* more recently, have been preparing to play a greater role as pressure groups, capable of negotiating collective interests ranging from the protection of social and cultural rights to the actions to be taken against xenophobia. Relying, at least rhetorically, on the role played by the economy in redefining German identity after the War, they also trust their ability to become a political power in the same way.

Should economic success be considered as a way of appropriating the "economic miracle" for the hope that prosperity and well-being thus provided will give a new content to the nation's identity and move it beyond the ethnic references? Or does this approach rather link the interpretation of citizenship to another, not less traditional status of the medieval bourgeois (*Bürger*)? In Germany, this second vision of citizenship refers more to belonging to civil society than to the political community. Civil society, in turn, is actually considered to be a bourgeois society (*die bürgerliche Gesellschaft*), which not only has to be distinguished from the state and its institutions, but even stands in opposition to them. Accordingly, every individual taking part in public life which is subject to economic competition can be considered a citizen. This suggests that the citizen is synonymous with the bourgeois, as "two sides of the same coin" (Dahrendorf 1988: p. 34). One might perhaps interpret the term *ausländische Mitbürger* (foreign co-citizen) in this light: a term introduced by the Greens and used frequently to express the acceptance of Turkish members of German society through their economic citizenship, in the absence of political citizenship. Can

we therefore see in their "embourgeoisment" a step toward naturalization (as suggested by the German term *Einbürgerung*), even if it is used
in reference to the State (*Staatsbürger*) and not to the city, as in the case
of the bourgeois? This very specific conception of citizenship puts the
economy in the service of politics and lends a political weight to the
Turks in Germany, who as a result are citizens without really being citizens because they still cannot be categorized as full citizens as defined
by the Constitution, that is citizens by descent.[12]

After World War II, the notion of citizenship was reconsidered,
notably by T. H. Marshall, in terms of social class, thereby extending
its legal and political content to the social dimension of equality before
the law.[13] But such a conception of citizenship describes social rights as
a continuity of political rights. Thus, "social citizenship," which inte-
grates the foreigner into existing corporatist structures, derives at this
level from direct participation in civil society. In Habermas' words, this
is "passive citizenship:" a citizenship legitimized by the development of
the welfare state that promotes equal access to social advantages and
grants the same constitutional protection in the area of human rights
that is enjoyed by the nationals. This type of participation is only indirect with regard to the political (or "active") element of citizenship.
Full integration into the political community becomes possible only by
holding a citizenship of legal and political status, which is granted
through "naturalization:" a process that takes into account such factors as the duration of residence, contribution of work and service, and
conformity to social norms. Joseph Carens (1998: pp. 141–9) argues
that one of the most relevant requirements for naturalization is fulfilled
by the individual's ambition in relation to the national society's
expectations.

Dual nationality or the construction of a national minority

Since 1990, the debate on citizenship in Germany has focused on the
question of dual nationality. Keeping one's original nationality has
become the mode of negotiating citizenship. These negotiations are
carried on with every new government. In 1999, the new coalition
government of the German Social Democratic Party (SPD) and the
Greens proposed that Turks keep their original nationality while
obtaining German nationality, which would mean the removal of the
constitutional article of renunciation. This proposal soon became the
focal point in the debate on citizenship, especially in relation to the
question of national identity and respect for the Constitution. It
caused, on one side, the opposition parties – the Christian Democratic

Union of Germany (CDU) and the Christian Social Union (CSU) of Bavaria – to collect signatures against its implementation, and on the other side, politically active Turkish immigrants to reclaim dual nationality as a condition for access to German citizenship. The law passed in January 2000 enables the child of a foreigner to acquire German nationality at birth, while maintaining the parental nationality. But, between the ages of 18 and 23, he or she will have to choose between the two nationalities, that is between remaining German and becoming a "foreigner."

The issue of dual nationality questions the relationship of citizenship to nationality and identity. In the case of Turks, identity would refer to their original nationality, while citizenship to their status in the host country, including the right of permanent residence, of protection against racism, and of political equality. Consequently, citizenship becomes a way of guaranteeing endowment of rights within the territory, but does not ensure cultural integration. In this perspective, citizenship constitutes no more than a simple juridical status, while nationality refers only to ethnicity, religion, and/or culture: whereas, in nation-states, nationality and citizenship are interdependent concepts. This actually constitutes a process of minority building.[14] In the case of Turks, the "minority" position relies on both Turkish national identity and Islamic religious identity; a national minority defined through its juridical status as foreigners, and a religious minority through the absence of Islam's institutional recognition in relation to other religions that have official status based on public law.

But what is the state's role in the construction of minorities? Part of the answer is given by the politics of integration, called *Ausländerpolitik*. Indeed, German public authorities affirm that they would like to see the Turkish nationals organize themselves in ethnic communities that are united by common interests beyond ideological, religious, ethnic, and linguistic cleavages. The objective declared by the Commission of Foreigners (*Ausländerbeauftragte*) is to help the immigrant populations, especially Turks, to establish organizations to represent a "community based on consensus" rather than see a multitude of formal or informal groups in conflict. While for political authorities this is about taking action against the foreigners' marginalization in the social, cultural, economic, and political realms, and helping them to reassemble in unified and solidary communities, such as those of the Church, for the foreigners themselves it becomes the only way to gain legitimacy and the recognition of their permanent presence in Germany.

Accordingly, the active members of these associations take the discourse of the public authorities seriously and they readily follow instructions to get organized or to form such communities. They assemble their forces to create an umbrella organization (*Dachorganisation*, i.e. a federation of associations in every *Land*, as well as at the federal level) with a view to regrouping the totality of Turkish members.[15] Thus, what the public authorities call "ethnic communities" resonates as the idea of "ethnic minority" on the part of the associations' leaders or other politically active individuals among the Turkish immigrants in Germany. What is meant by this term is the structural presence of a culturally different population of nearly two million individuals of all social categories (workers, both qualified and non-qualified, students, employees, businessmen, industrialists, artists, intellectuals), who express their affiliation to different regional, linguistic, or ethnic cultures: a *türkische Minderheit* (Turkish minority), as suggested by members of the SPD, a notion that emphasizes the nationality of the home country as the basis for the creation of a minority. The constant reminder that German national identity is founded on descent might actually be the reason for non-Germans to consider themselves in a similar way, that is to identify with ethnic criteria such as their former nationality. Or is it the political environment and the juridical status that maintain the differences between the nationalities as constitutive elements in the creation of a collective identity, and even in its institutionalization as a minority?

The Turkish state contributes as much as the German state to the formation of a nationally based ethnic minority in Germany. Its primary interest here lies in the creation of a Turkish "lobby" in order to defend the image and interests of Turkey in Germany, as well as in Europe, especially vis-à-vis supranational institutions. These distinctive strategies can be found more in representations than in the modes of organization. Whether ethnic community, national minority, or Turkish lobby, they all refer to a structure centered on the notion of a nationality with common interests and identity. Doesn't one also see here the echo of the desire of successive governments to see the "guests" return to their home country some day, and thus to send them back to "their state" as the only refuge and source of security and rights, as if to remind them of the principle of access to German citizenship as being primarily based on a common cultural heritage?

This does not prevent the minority from defining itself through its relation to the German state, the only legitimate structure to define the limits of its recognition. The strategies of compensation by associative engagement and incorporation into civil society display a willingness for integration into the political society, but only by means of the communal structures that are available. Paradoxically, these same structures lead immigrants to distance themselves by expressing attachment to their inherited nationality and demanding its recognition. The demand for dual nationality finds itself rooted precisely in this contradiction in the so-called politics for foreigners (*Ausländerpolitik*): the recognition of communal affiliations inscribed in the structures of society. As a result, citizenship and civil engagement are confined within a restricted group, without access to the larger political community and without links to the community of the neighborhood or other foreign populations in the country. But at the same time, given the practice of citizenship as political, juridical, social, economic, and its content of identity as cultural or legal, the combination corresponds to a feeling of loyalty directed simultaneously at the group, community, civil society, and the state. It is their interpenetration that accounts for the strategies of the actors and their demand for dual citizenship.

Moreover, the political language contains a vocabulary that distinguishes citizenship from nationality and identity. Both citizenship (*Staatsbürgerschaft*) and nationality (*Staatsangehörigkeit*) refer to the state; but the first does so in instrumental terms, while the second, in terms of belonging. The reference to dual citizenship (*die doppelte Staatsbürgerschaft*) has a basis in this duality, which is actually internally complementary: the construction of an ethnic (national) minority in Germany, with a citizen-identity that emphasizes political and institutional assimilation. This analysis opposes the pessimistic theses that emphasize the "delay in assimilation" that might be caused by maintaining the nationality of the home country.[16] On the contrary, the dual citizenship demanded by the Turks could be perceived as a right that would permit the negotiation of a moral, ethno-national personality that is based on a triple reference: (a) to German civil society, by residence, with the civil rights and duties that are linked to it; (b) to Turkish nationality, in terms of identity (for those who identify themselves with it) and experiences that lead to a reinforcement of belonging to the community; and (c) to the German state. It is this multiplicity that is at stake in the citizenship to be negotiated.

For those groups who are promoting a specific identity, the willingness to integrate into the political community by demanding citizenship and maintaining an "attachment" to the original nationality may be understood as a way out of political marginality. It therefore expresses a struggle for emancipation. But, in contrast to the emancipation of the Age of Enlightenment, where religion was separated from public life and individuals from their communities in order to ensure their primordial *identification* with the nation, dual citizenship can be based on the willingness to participate with equal rights that also recognize religious or communal identities inscribed in the structural framework of the state.

However, the terminological and conceptual distinctions in reference to the state, which remain as sources of ambiguity, are echoed in the hesitations about how to name those foreigners who in the meantime have grown roots in the national territory. They are called "non-Germans" by the liberal Right and "foreign co-citizens" by the Greens, who aim to stress their positive contribution to society; and, finally, there is the notion of the *Türken mit Deutschem Pass* (Turks with a German passport) for the more than 250,000 persons who immigrated from Turkey and are now naturalized Germans. These people already constitute an important electoral potential, and the parties compete for finding a place for them within the political community. A study on the electoral behaviour of the Turks in 1994 has revealed that, if they had been German citizens at the time, 49 percent would have voted for the SPD, compared with 67 percent in 1986, 11 percent for the Greens, 10 percent for the FDP (Free Democratic Party), and 6 percent for the CDU. Although the number of German citizen voters of Turkish origin, aged 18 and above, is no more than 35,000, the advertisements that the political parties place in community journals resemble a sort of electoral investment. The FDP counts on Turkish votes to pass the 5 percent threshold for entering the parliament, and the SPD supports their leading associations in order to prevent their members from adhering to other parties (Sen and Karakasoglu 1994).

These expressions and approaches bring to light the link that could be made or unmade between citizens and nationals. Dividing the electorate on the basis of nationality (nationality of origin, or dual nationality) demonstrates the difficulty that the public opinion and the political class have in accepting the "foreigners" as part of the nation. Rather than limiting identification with the ethnic community in civil society, an approach founded on dual nationality establishes a duality between minority status and citizenship in the political community.

Toward a new unity of Germany

Hence, the real question must be one of citizenship, and not of dual citizenship. Whereas the latter calls for a re-examination of the concept of the state and its relationship to the definition of the nation, citizenship implies an opportunity for the individual to participate in the national political community. Furthermore, dual citizenship does not imply participation in two political spaces simultaneously. A citizen is an active citizen of only one state, where he or she fully exercises his or her rights and duties. The process of naturalization, by which the individual becomes a member of a political community, assures integration. Of course, this process is subject to certain conditions, but they only concern the relationship between the individual and his or her *new political community* within the framework of the state, hence within a circumscribed territory. Clearly, this need not be accompanied by cultural amnesia or completely forgetting about a former affiliation of nationality or citizenship; but the latter now constitutes only a document reserved to private life. Finally, its juridical validity simply depends on agreements made between the states. As a consequence, the argument about "the democratic influence" (Spiro 1999) of dual citizenship, that is of the utilization in the country of origin of the constitutional values acquired in the Western democracies, has only limited significance.

The construction of Europe brings about the creation of networks of transnational solidarities that challenge the nation-state. But even though these networks seek to bypass national politics, it is, in reality, ultimately within the states of citizenship that the limits of recognition of differences are negotiated and, thus, the expressions of identities admitted (Kastoryano 1997: pp. 59–67). These negotiations aim at elaborating new codes of coexistence by redefining certain values or reinforcing others, so that the "idea" of a uniform nation-state is combined with the "de facto" pluralism of modern societies, and its institutional representations, in order to ensure a historical continuity and to recognize the particularities that emerge in the public sphere: in short, to re-establish the link between the state and civil society, and achieve a redefinition of the social and political pact. It is a question of a balance between civil society and the state, or of a link between cultural diversity and citizenship, where neither civic principles nor the collectivity's ultimate identity are affected.

Focusing the debates on, and mobilizing emotions around, the issue of dual nationality can only contribute to the continuation of the idea of an "elsewhere," inserted into the political community, and to the reinforcement of the notion of a national minority with a distinct identity, where the status of foreigner is maintained in spite of legal accession to citizenship.[17] This results in the distinction between the true and the false citizen. Although dual nationality can be perceived as a temporary and pragmatic means of inclusion into the political community, especially with a rhetoric based on citizenship, making it the touchstone of a debate on the desired changes in citizenship laws, even if the laws guarantee equal rights, causes a return to the separation of "nationalities," renders a permanent and structural quality to the status of foreigner, and precludes assimilation.

Granting the right to acquire German nationality to children born to foreign parents in Germany clearly constitutes an important step toward the acceptance of the "other," but only provided that mentalities open up along with the institutional changes: and this would be thanks to social and political discourse, and the discourse in the media, which would help the immigrants, that is the new citizens, to identify with the state and its institutions. It would be difficult to conceive of a democratic state without any dimension of identification (Taylor 1992: pp. 135–53).

Perhaps more than other nations, Germany is exposed to the scrutiny of public opinion, due to a past whose wounds have not yet been healed. The laws on nationality should not thwart the long development of democracy that Germany has seen since the end of the War and delay its process of "reconciliation" with other democratic states. The real challenge for Germany today is therefore to encourage an identification of its "new citizens" with the German institutions, its fundamental principles, and its constitution, and to help them develop a feeling of responsibility vis-à-vis political life and their new "community of destiny," founded upon a new political unity, and, finally, to affirm itself as a nation-state in Europe.

Notes

1 These children will also acquire their parents' citizenship, under the principle of descent, and will have to decide, between the ages of 18 and 23, which citizenship they will retain, as they will be unable to retain both.
2 For the convergence of the laws of citizenship, see Weil and Hansen (1999).
3 Discourse of Fichte, taken up by A. Renaut.
4 His ambitions and intentions are described in a work that he wrote in 1992 (see Cohn-Bendit and Schmid 1992).
5 In 1993, the number of applications for naturalization reached 44,950; and they have continued to increase since then (see Schmidt and Weick 1999: pp. 267–76; Münz and Ulrich 1998: pp. 25–56).
6 *La lettre de la citoyenneté*, no. 31, January-February 1998.
7 On citizenship as a feeling of belonging and citizenship as engagement, see Jean Leca (1986: pp. 159–213).
8 This has led Peter Katzenstein (1987: pp. 168–92) to refer to the German state as a "semi-sovereign state." See also Sheri Berman (1997: pp. 562–74).
9 In 1989, the Constitutional Court rejected the foreigners' right to vote in local elections, which was granted by the Parliament of Hamburg in 1987. The reason put forward was that (as in Article 3 of the French Constitution) the right to vote in local and federal elections can only be acquired with the possession of German nationality. Thus, foreigners still remain outside of the framework of electoral participation.
10 Migration News Sheet, Bruxelles, December 1991, cited in Zentrum für Türkeistudien (1993).

11 Statistics of the Union of the Turkish Entrepreneurs of Berlin. See also: Zentrum für Türkeistudien (1992).
12 Gosewinkel (1998). The author points out that the democratic Constitution of Weimar Germany (1919) envisaged a civil society with equal rights for men and women, and upheld a definition of the legal status of citizenship as affiliation to the state. This law was abolished in 1935 by the law of Nürnberg.
13 Marshall (1964). The author draws attention to the extension of social practices of citizenship to other domains such as health, education, and access to social welfare in general.
14 In the German context, the concept of "minority" is actually reserved for those Germans who had a minority status after going into exile during World War II. This explains why the same notion has been rejected for today's immigrants.
15 As, for example, the *Türkische Gemeinde zu Berlin*. The example is taken from the *jüdische Gemeinde zu Berlin* (the Jewish Community of Berlin) where it seems (rhetorically as well as in practice) as if the activists want to display the good relations between Turkey and Israel. More importantly, it also represents a way to show their openness towards other communities or minorities. Even more importantly, however, it is as if the association wants to prove to the German public, as well as to its own members, its efforts in the realm of "minority" building, in accordance with a certain "minority type," and to make them sensitive to the common fight against racism which can only be emphasized by supporting Jewish organizations.
16 Argument developed by Peter H. Schuck (1998).
17 It has to be noted, however, that *Aussiedler*, who are naturalized as soon as they arrive in Germany, maintain the nationality of their countries of departure (Poland, Romania, or even the Republics of Central Asia). See Münz and Ulrich (1998).

3 Greece

Religion, nation, and membership in the European Union

Effie Fokas

The Orthodox Church of Greece has historically played a powerful role as preserver of national identity, a fact which translated into an intense interplay between Church and State. In contemporary terms, the Church struggles to maintain both its role as preserver of national identity, and its strong position vis-à-vis the State. This struggle results, in many cases, in a tension between the Greek nation-state and the European Union (EU), due to the norms advanced by the latter in terms of religious freedoms. The historical relationship between religion and national identity in Greece is well documented in the scholarly literature. A brief overview of certain climactic periods or events in the course of its development, however, will help us to understand how this relationship has led to the contemporary links between religion, nation, and European norms.

The background to all this is the status of the Orthodox Church during Ottoman rule. Under the Ottoman *millet* system, the Patriarch of Constantinople was recognized as the highest religious and political leader (*millet bashi*) of all Orthodox peoples (regardless of ethnicity) living within the Ottoman Empire. The entailed privileges and responsibilities were immense: the Patriarch and higher clergy were themselves exempted from taxes, but they were responsible for collecting them from the Orthodox *millet* for the Islamic state and for guaranteeing their subjects' full obedience to the Sultan. The *millet* system also granted the Patriarchate full juridical authority over the Orthodox (on matters of marriage, dowry, property, inheritance, education, and social welfare). Thus, with this vast expanse of functions, the Church was legitimized by the Ottoman state as a religio-political institution (Kokosalakis 1995: pp. 239–40; Makrides 1991: p. 284; Dimitropoulos 2001: p. 52).

Though the Orthodox *millet* was an ecumenical and multinational setting, in reality it was largely Greek-dominated: the succession of

Patriarchs was Greek, and the social administration was almost exclusively in the hands of Greeks, since the *Phanariots* (the Greek population living in Constantinople) were already the leaders of business there and had become directly involved in the administration of the Ottoman Empire itself. In the Ottoman social system, Greek ethnic identity and the Orthodox (or *Rum*) *millet* had become identical (Roudometof 2001: pp. 53–4). Furthermore, with a Greek Patriarch carrying out secular and ecclesiastical functions, and a largely Greek hierarchy in control of the Orthodox *millet*, "Greek interests came to dominate a Church that became increasingly involved in the preservation and perpetuation of Hellenism and it became more and more difficult to separate Hellenism from Orthodoxy" (Rexine 1972: p. 201). Indeed, the Church was the only institution which provided for national Greek education by establishing schools, printing presses, scholarships, and food for school children. It was thus the chief educational and social instrument of the Greeks in the Ottoman world that secured them from Islamization. Accordingly, beyond the institutional role of the Church, in its economic, legal, and political dimensions, one must also note the important psychological function it had for the Greeks under Ottoman rule: the Church was seen as provider and protector of the people and preserver of their national identity.

Religion and national identity

The Church's efforts to preserve Greek national identity did not mean, however, that it was willing to "revive the Greek nation." The Church was in a highly comfortable position under Ottoman rule. Besides the aforementioned power and privileges, the Church also became especially wealthy: many Christians transmitted their land to the Church and the monasteries since, under the *millet* system, ecclesiastical property was protected from confiscation by the Turks (Kokosalakis 1995: p. 240). Therefore, the high clergy were not entirely supportive of revolutionary ideas which might threaten their relatively privileged positions. Furthermore, as education and Grecophone secular literary production expanded in the post-1750 period, the re-emergence of classical antiquity in the discourse of the Western Enlightenment reached the *Rum millet* and strongly influenced its secularization. The ecclesiastical establishment and many Phanariots opposed these new ideas since they correctly perceived that secularization would shift the religious foundation of solidarity among the members of the *Rum millet* and lead to the de-legitimization of the Church and the Phanariots. Meanwhile, proponents of "enlightened reason" accused the Church of "voluntary slavery" (Roudometof 2001: pp. 56–61). Thus, a major ideological conflict developed between much of the hierarchy and Greek population on the one hand, and the Western-minded individuals seeking Greek national independence on the other.

In addition to contradictory perspectives on the role of the Church in the revolution, there are also conflicting interpretations of the meaning of the revolution. According to the theologian Evangelos Theodorou, for example, the revolution of 1821 "was a lawful, and holy, war declared by the Greek Nation against a foreign conqueror, under whose rule, the life of free citizens was not tolerated."[1] The prevailing view amongst historians, however, is that the revolution was national, not religious.[2] As Dimitropoulos argues, beyond a rebellion against Ottoman legality, the revolution also included an element of denial of the power of the central Church: a reluctance to submit to a religious leader chosen by and required to submit to the tyrant. Accordingly, religion was being transformed, from a politically charged distinction between Muslims and the rest of Christians, into a cultural characteristic of the new identity of those who had rebelled against the Ottomans. The religious leaders were supposed henceforth to serve the *political* aims of the struggle, and the Church itself would be barred from political power.

Regardless of the perspective on whether it was a "holy" war or not, the symbolic importance of those clergy who did fight for Greek independence remains embedded in the memories, and historical chronicles, of many. This was not because of any revolutionary role of the Church during the Greek uprising, "but because she was and continues to be a Church tied to the ethnic identity of the Greeks."[3] It is thus that one of the most renowned aspects of the revolution is the act of a Greek bishop, Germanos of Patra, who on 25 March 1821 raised as the banner (*lavaron*) of revolution the curtain of the sanctuary of the cathedral of Patras (Rexine 1972: p. 203). And it is thus that 25 March is now celebrated as Greek National Independence Day. So in spite of conflicting perspectives on the attitudes and actions of the clergy throughout the national revolution, the prevailing interpretation in school books and in popular opinion is that the Church saved the Greek nation throughout the four centuries of Ottoman rule, and that there would have been no "nation" to rebel against the Ottomans had the Church not played this role. It therefore remains unquestionable that in this period an especially strong link between Orthodoxy and national identity was consolidated. The Greek national revolution, then, constitutes the first climactic episode in the relationship between the national and religious identities.

Following the National Revolution, the second climactic point in the developing relationship between Greek Orthodoxy and national identity was the establishment of the Autocephalous Church of Greece and its eventual recognition by the Ecumenical Patriarchate. Newly independent Greece was ruled by the regency of the young Bavarian King Otto, who was installed by the Great Powers (Britain, France, and Russia). Georg von Mauer, the member of the regency responsible for issues of Church, Education, and Justice, believed that complete political independence for Greece required a disentanglement of the Church from the Ecumenical Patriarchate. Contact of the Church with foreign centers of decision-making was deemed contrary to the interests of the new political leadership. Thus, in spite of the Patriarch's staunch protests, the Autocephalous Church of Greece was proclaimed by royal decree in July 1833.

The declaration of autonomy from the Ecumenical Patriarchate also entailed legalization of the Church's subordination to the state. The administrative leader of the highest ecclesiastical power, a five-member Synod, was to be the King (though Roman Catholic). The latter was in accordance with the Bavarian prototype whereby the King was also the "supreme bishop" (Kokosalakis 1987: p. 235; Frazee 1979: p. 90). The members of the Synod were to be hired by the government, and a royal commissioner would represent civil power at each of its meetings.[4] Thus, the 1833 decree of "The Independence of the Church of Greece" made the State the exclusive legislative ruler and declared the Church subject to the monarch. This was later institutionalized in the Constitution of 1844, Article 105, stipulating that Church administration matters would be regulated by the State (Papastathis 1995: pp. 75–92).

Despite its declared intention to modernize the Church and to improve the educational standard of the clergy, the monarchy proceeded instead to execute policies aimed only at limiting the assets of the Church. The most vivid example of this consists in the second wave of Church subjugation by the State: an attack on the monasteries and their properties. By an 1833 royal decree, 412 of the existing 593 monasteries were closed down, and their properties were confiscated and passed to the Crown. In some cases the monastery closures took violent form, with the Bavarian army forcefully expelling the monks for placement in the remaining monasteries (Kokosalakis 1987: p. 236; Roudometof 2001: p. 103). Finally, a royal decree also forbade any future gifts of land estate to the Church. The strict measures were, according to Dimitropoulos (2001: p. 60), an effort to dissolve important sources of power which could become centers of resistance to State policy. But of course these developments incited a great deal of discontent, both within the clergy and amongst the wider population.

Assessing the significance of the establishment of the Autocephalous Church is difficult. The literal *creation* of the Autocephalous Church by the State clearly signals the radical beginning of Church subordination to State interests (Manitakis 2000: pp. 328–31). But the consequent relationship between Church and State is complex: while the right of the State to interfere in ecclesiastical matters was legalized, ecclesiastical issues were recognized as public issues. In other words, as Dimitropoulos (2001: p. 61) points out, the autocephaly did entail subjugation of the Church and thus the affirmation and institutionalization of liberal ideas, but it also entailed the paradox that, "as political power became disentangled from religion, the Church became bound to the State." Most importantly, in spite of the fact that, for the clergy and a small proportion of the population, the establishment of the Autocephalous Church was a negative development, the newly independent Church did become a widely recognized symbol of national identity and thus enhanced the ethnic character of the Church. Particularly the fact that its establishment was a revolutionary act (i.e. a split from the Patriarchate without its consent) meant for most Greeks that the Autocephaly was the attainment of the fullest extent of national independence and national identity.

Following the establishment of the Autocephalous Church, the next climactic point in our historical overview is the repairing of relations with the Patriarchate and the latter's official recognition of the Autocephalous Church of Greece. Due to unease over the State's extensive control over the Church, its ensuing attacks on monasteries, and its failure to "protect" the Church and nation from "threats" of other faiths, many clergy and lay people began to call for renewed relations with the Patriarchate (Dimitropoulos 2001: p. 62). Conservatives sought a reunion with the Church of Constantinople and security against the proselytizing efforts of other faiths, whilst liberals sought the constitutional substantiation of the Autocephalous Church and the separation of Church and State. The ideological debate between the two factions initially resulted in the formulation in the 1844 Constitution, whereby Eastern Orthodoxy was recognized as the "prevailing" faith that "existed" in dogmatic union with the Church of Constantinople. In the context of common compromise, the King ceased to be the head of the Church and its administration was left to a Synod of hierarchs. The Church remained under the control of the State and its holy canons were applied to the extent that they were not contrary to the canons of the State. Finally, all acts of proselytism committed "against" Orthodoxy were strictly prohibited.

Conservative factions of society remained unsatisfied, however, and the clergy in particular continued to request normalization of relations with the Patriarchate.[5] Thus, as a further concession, the Greek government issued a formal request to the Patriarchate for its recognition of the Church of Greece as Autocephalous. The Patriarchate, for its part, was favorable towards anything that might strengthen its role, because the gradual proliferation of national Churches across the Balkans had threatened to render it powerless. Thus, in 1850, the Patriarchate officially recognized the Autocephalous Church of Greece.[6] The recognition was greeted with great enthusiasm by political and ecclesiastical circles. Beyond repairing relations of both the Greek Church and State with the Patriarchate, the move also normalized Church–State relations internally to Greece. The official recognition of the Autocephalous Church clearly added ideological strength to the national aspirations and ethnic ideology of the Greek state (Kokosalakis 1987: p. 239).

The next period under examination is that of Greek irredentist policy and the *Megali idea* (or "Grand Idea"). Here the aims of the state for its expansion coincided with the visions of religious nationalists for the "redemption" of Orthodox peoples: visions which were expressed with reference to Byzantine glory. The doctrine of the *Megali idea* was first articulated in 1844 by the politician John Kolettis, as a romantic vision of re-establishing modern Greece with its pre-Ottoman occupation boundaries, that is reclaiming all the Hellenic lands of the Classical and Byzantine eras. The King fervently advocated the vision, as did most of the Greek people (Kokosalakis 1987: p. 238). The manifestation of this idea in government policy, and the tragic events which effectively brought it to an end in 1922, when the Greek army was defeated by Turkish nationalists, are well documented in historical texts. The "Asia Minor crisis" is, indeed, one of the most critical turning points in Greek history, and a clear product of the blending of millenarianism with nationalism, and of Orthodoxy with Greek national identity.

Whereas there are conflicting interpretations with regard to the relationship among Church, State, and national identity throughout Ottoman rule, the revolution, and the establishment of Autocephaly, there is general agreement that the *Megali idea* acted as an ultimate synthesis of Church, State, and national identity. Put together, the three historical facts of the establishment of the Autocephalous Church, its recognition by the Patriarchate, and the development of the *Megali idea* introduce us to certain trends which we see repeated throughout the history of modern Greece: first, the tendency of the State to compromise in the face of Church demands; second, the tendency of the State to use the Church and Orthodoxy as expedient factors of national unity; and third, the tendency of the Church to identify itself with such national causes.

Most notably, we see these trends repeated nearly a century later: during the 1967–74 military dictatorship. The most important aspect of this period for our purposes is the interaction between the dictators and the Church. This, together with the particular violence which characterized this military regime, carried long-term effects on the relationship between Orthodoxy and national identity in Greece. The military coup of 21 April 1967 took place under the pretext that there was a danger of communist takeover in Greece, following a bitter civil war between conservatives and leftists. On the morning of the coup, the army arrested most major political leaders and persons classified as "suspects, potentially dangerous or known enemies" (Kent 1971: p. 384).[7] Approximately 5,000 people were incarcerated before dawn.

As George Kent rightly notes, however, it is one thing to execute a *coup d'état* and quite another to legitimize the new regime. The junta operated on the premise that the overthrow would be legitimized if they had the backing of the Church and the monarchy. For his part, the King refused to sign a document endorsing the new government. In their efforts to lure the Church into their camp, the generals argued that they would benefit Greece with a moral regeneration based upon devotion to Greek nationalism, anti-communism, and the Orthodox Church (Frazee 1979: p. 91). Indeed, amongst the various orientations the junta could have taken, they chose a "traditionalistic revival" type of regime. The purpose of education was henceforth to be "the cultivation of nationalistic and Christian conscience of students." Texts would be revised to include "particular stress on history and religion," because "Greece is surrounded by communists and Slavs" (*The New York Times* 19 May 1967: p. 38). The colonels' call for the "purification" and "regeneration" of Greece, and "Puritan morality," was reinforced by a strict dress code: the wearing of mini-skirts was forbidden, and men were not allowed to have long hair or beards (*The New York Times* 25 April 1967: p. 1). Furthermore, the colonels enforced severe censorship,[8] and even tried to control the religious practices of the citizens: all government officials were required to attend church weekly, and all school children, civil servants, and leftists under police supervision were required to take Holy Communion once a week. Other citizens were not obliged to attend church, but were urged to do so in order to "build a nation of Christian Greeks." Anyone who publicly doubted the existence of God could be arrested and found guilty of blasphemy (Kent 1971: p. 401).[9]

Specifically in terms of the junta's relations with the Church, amongst the first moves of the new "theocratic–puritanical" (Yiannaras 1976: p. 116) government was to interfere in Church affairs. The regime forced the acting archbishop to retire and altered the process by which bishops and archbishops would henceforth be elected, allowing for the dictators (rather than the Holy Synod) to make the final decision. This historical period, marked as it was by the junta's motto "Greece of Christian Greeks," carried inestimable long-term effects on the relationship between the Church and national identity. First, the perception that the Church serves the interests of the powers-that-be was strengthened. But of course, the stronger lasting sentiment was that the Church did so uncritically, and that it worked in close cooperation with an undemocratic, violent leadership. There lingered in public life, after the 1974 return to democracy, what one scholar describes as "a kind of repugnance which is usually expressed with the phrase 'let the priests destroy themselves'" (Yiannaras 1976: pp. 132–9). Even the contemporary Church is often seen through this historical prism. A 2001 newspaper research article subtitled "The black page of the ecclesiastical hierarchy which doesn't seem to close," was dedicated to demonstrating that the Church was as involved in politics as ever during the dictatorship, and not least Christodoulos, who acted as secretary of the Holy Synod in that period (*Eleutherotypia* 22 May 2001).

In fact, the election of Christodoulos to the archbishopric may be considered another climactic point in the relationship between Greek Orthodoxy and national identity. Many scholars have noted a significant change in the role of the Church in Greek society with the advent of Archbishop Christodoulos in 1998. The increased involvement of the Church in secular issues under his leadership has been the subject of countless newspaper articles and academic publications. We will thus limit our examination to the general point that Archbishop Christodoulos introduced a new strong emphasis on national identity to ecclesiastical discourse.

It is important that such tendencies be viewed through the prism of the weakening role of the nation-state in general, and more precisely, the Greek state's trend towards de-nationalization, in terms of identifying itself more with the supranational EU dimension. In this context, the Church (or, more precisely, powerful elements within the Church hierarchy) actively claims a special role in maintaining a national identity which, some feel, is being compromised by the State. A second important dimension here is the increasingly multi-ethnic nature of Greek society, and the pressure exerted by the EU in terms of the latter's demands for enhanced religious freedoms and equality for non-Orthodox citizens of Greece. Thus, in the light of the State's efforts to conform to EU standards, following many European Court of Human Rights (ECHR) convictions,[10] many Church leaders perceive a heightened threat to the cultural, linguistic, and religious homogeneity of Greece: all elements which are central to conceptions of Greek national identity.

We see references to these worries in the rhetoric of Archbishop Christodoulos. One example will suffice to show that, while his speech is not explicitly anti-European, he portrays the EU as the reason for the critical need to focus on the role of Orthodoxy in national identity. In a speech delivered in 1999, he bemoans the fact that modern Greeks have ceased to perceive of the clergy as their representative and "guarantor of their Hellenicity."[11] After going on to explain the crimes committed by the West against Greek Orthodoxy after the Greek revolution, the fact that the roots of the European integration project were Christian Democratic and, specifically, Catholic, he states:

> We are in a crisis in the evolution of Hellenism ... our big problem is the duration of Hellenism ... if we want not only to re-establish our spiritual identity, but to play a role as Greeks in the EU of values and not only of capital and interests, we have but one recourse: to re-load ourselves with our historical baggage, which is our Greco-Orthodoxy ...

Church–State relations

Archbishop Christodoulos is likewise vocal on perceived threats to Church–State relations. In a speech delivered soon after his election in 1998, he referred to those who wish to change the status quo in Church–State relations as *graeculi,* meaning those who are servile toward everything foreign and thus undeserving of Greek identity and lead to its decay: such people wish to reduce the Church's role "because they know that the nation owes its survival to the Church."[12] But before addressing the Church's effort to maintain its powerful position vis-à-vis the State, we must first consider the factors which led to this powerful position.

A preliminary factor is the constitutional status of the Church. Article 3 of the Greek Constitution establishes the Eastern Orthodox faith as the "prevailing" faith. It is in the inherent privileges granted to the Church through this Article that we may best understand its strong standing in relation to the State. The wording of this constitutional provision is problematic: it is unclear whether the term "prevailing" indicates a statement of fact (i.e. that the faith is shared by approximately 97 percent of the population in Greece), or whether the term entails a normative statement (i.e. that Orthodoxy ought to be the prevailing religion, and is thus deserving of protective privileges). The former is the predominant view amongst constitutional specialists and within Greek courts. But there is a great deal of debate over whether, regardless of constitutional terminology and predominant interpretations, in practice the faith is treated as if it ought to prevail in Greece, thus granting the Orthodox Church of Greece privileges vis-à-vis the State and over other faiths represented in the country (Alivizatos 1999: p. 25).

In terms of privileges vis-à-vis the State, the clergy of the Orthodox Church of Greece are remunerated and pensioned by the State: the State pays the salaries and pensions of the clergy, the preachers and lay employees of the Orthodox Church, and the Church is exempted from taxation.[13] Furthermore, Metropolitans are given a role in the issuance of licenses for the building of places of worship for minority faiths. Religion lessons in public schools reflect the opinions of the Orthodox clergy. State holidays are based on the religious calendar, so that the holidays of the Greek Orthodox Church are acknowledged as official national holidays. Significantly, National Independence Day, 25 March, is also a major religious holiday (the Annunciation of Mary). Also significant is the fact that the Statutory Charter of the Church must be passed by the Plenary Session of Parliament (Konidaris 2003: pp. 227–8). Meanwhile, the Archbishop presides over each opening session of parliament and blesses each of the parliamentarians with Holy Water. Of especially symbolic impact is the fact that Church and State leaders often jointly preside over State functions and national holiday celebrations. Finally, one cannot underestimate the role of politicians themselves in entrenching such Church–State links through their own presence in and contributions to religious functions.[14] Each of these facts, in varying degrees, entails an especially close relationship between Church and State in Greece.

The privileges accorded, in Article 3, to the Orthodox Church vis-à-vis other faiths are more important for our purposes, as the State's efforts to minimize these privileges, in conformity with European norms, have been a serious point of contention between Church and State. Some of the privileges enjoyed by the Orthodox Church entail restrictions on religious freedoms of non-Orthodox citizens and limitations on the principle of equality. These restrictions raise problems with regard to Greece's status as a signatory to the European Charter for Human Rights. We identify here three domains of the Orthodox Church's privileges in particular: the building and operation of places of worship for non-Orthodox peoples in Greece; the application of legal provisions against proselytism; and the aim and content of the religious courses in public schools. A fourth issue, that of the inclusion of religious persuasion on the national identity cards, will be discussed at length below.

It is a 1939 law, enacted under the Metaxas dictatorship, which determines the rights of minority faiths to build churches and operate places of worship (Alivizatos 1999: p. 33). According to this law, beyond the usual building permit, the construction of any church or place of worship requires an application for permission submitted to the Minister of Education and Religious Affairs who, in turn, seeks the approval of the competent (relative to the district) Greek Orthodox bishop.[15] If a church is built without license, this is punishable with jail and the local Metropolitan has the right to call for the tearing down of the building. The approval of the local bishop is actually, in legal terms, an "opinion" which the Minister of Education and Religious Affairs is required to hear, but not to obey, in deciding on issuance of the permits. However, as one Greek bureaucrat confirms, the Minister rarely decides in opposition to the local bishop's "opinion" (Papastathis 1995: p. 85). In any case, this situation is clearly problematic in that the whole legal procedure of permit authorization gives the sense that all members of minority faith communities are, from the start, suspect and likely to act in ways which are antithetical to public order and upright morals (Dimitropoulos 2001: p. 139). Also, the discriminatory enforcement of this legislation by Greek authorities has, to this day, been the only case leading to unreserved condemnation of Greece by the ECHR for practices against religious minorities (Alivizatos 1999: p. 32). Thus, in reality, the general tendency today still gives priority to the safeguarding of the prevailing religion over actual religious freedom (Dimitropoulos 2001: p. 144).

The second problematic issue relates to legislation against proselytism. Although the 1975 Constitution extended the law against proselytism to protect all faiths and not solely Orthodoxy, the prevalent tendency is to use this legislation mainly to defend the Orthodox Church against the spread of other faiths in Greece (or, perhaps more precisely, against the threat of conversions from Orthodoxy to other faiths). This also has led to several indictments against the Greek state in the ECHR.[16] The operative legislation on proselytism also goes back to the time of the Metaxas dictatorship. Specifically, the definition of proselytism is set out in a 1939 law as "the attempt to intrude on the religious beliefs of a person of a different religious persuasion ... by taking advantage of his inexperience, trust, need, low intellect, or naivety."[17] Especially difficult here is the vague wording of the clause, which has allowed for extremely strict interpretation of specifically non-Orthodox actions. As Alivizatos notes, the mere distribution of pamphlets and brochures, and the mailing of books and periodicals, have led to prosecution and even to prison sentences.[18]

Finally, the religion courses in public schools are problematic on two fronts: with regard to Article 13 of the 1975 Constitution on freedom of conscience, and to Article 4 on the principle of equality. Article 16 (para. 2) sets out that the intention of education is, among other things, "the development of religious conscience of the Greeks." This decree does not explicitly call for a mandatory lesson in religion, nor that the development of religious conscience must be one-denominational and catechetical in character. But in its implementation, each of these is the case, thus putting into question guarantees of freedom of conscience. In primary and secondary education, the mandatory lesson *is* of catechetical character (although, we should note, it is only mandatory for Orthodox Christians; that is other-denominational students may be excused from the course upon provision of proof of other denominational status): the intention of the course, among other things, is to "help the students possess faith towards the fatherland and towards the genuine elements of the Orthodox Christian tradition."[19] In the case of tertiary education, the intention of the program includes development of the students' "awareness of the deeper importance of the Orthodox Christian ethos and of the stable dedication to pananthropic values."[20] According to Dimitropoulos (2001: p. 146), the aim of this religious education is neither to acquire knowledge about religious phenomena nor to understand the religious and cultural environment in which students live, but to make students good Christians, faithful members of the dominant religious community, and supportive of the perspectives of the Official Church.

Furthermore, the religion course raises questions concerning the principle of equality. A 1949 decision of the Council of State (StE) ruled that only Orthodox individuals could teach the course. Accordingly in primary schools, where there is only one teacher for all the subjects taught, a non-Orthodox teacher could not be hired (Papastathis 1995: pp. 83–4). In secondary schools, the exclusion of non-Orthodox teachers applied only to teachers of the religion course. In practice though, the administration resisted hiring non-Orthodox teachers even for the teaching of courses which had nothing to do with religion: "the non-Orthodox teacher was seen as suspect for proselytism ... since he was not enlightened by the 'truth of faith'" (Dimitropoulos 2001: p. 147). Against the staunch resistance of the Church, the law was changed in 1988 to allow for non-Orthodox teachers to be able to teach all subjects *except* religion. Both the nature of the religious courses and the rights of non-Orthodox teachers to assume the courses have recently come into examination by the StE.[21]

Clearly, it is not so much the formal constitutional establishment of the Orthodox Church of Greece as "prevailing" which is problematic, but the advantages to the Orthodox Church which exist in practice. These privileges continue to exist due, to a large degree, to the active efforts of the Church to maintain them. The historical relationship between religion and national identity, and the Church's consequent ability to play on the national sensitivities of the Greek population (97 percent Greek Orthodox), significantly enhance these efforts in the face of attempts by the state to limit the Church's privileges.

The "identity card crisis"

We now turn to examine one particular conflict between Church and State: that over the inclusion of reference to religion on the national identity cards. The identity card issue demonstrates how Greek membership in the EU may give rise to heightened efforts on the part of the Church to promote itself as protector of national identity which, in turn, breeds tension between the Church and the State. Our special interest is in how such tension may, in its final stage, influence Greece's place vis-à-vis the EU.

Greek citizens are required to carry with them at all times an identity card which is issued to them by the police. The inclusion of information regarding the citizen's religious orientation dates back to the 1936–40 Metaxas dictatorship: the official reason for this was the "strengthening of national religious convictions," and the unofficial reason was to ascertain who were the atheist communists in the country (or, furthermore, to compel those who were afraid to admit this to carry cards identifying them as Orthodox Christians). Later, under the Papadopoulos dictatorship, Legal Decree 127/1969 formally set out the details which were to be included on national identity cards, amongst which was religious affiliation. In 1986, discussion of the constitutionality of stating religious affiliation on a public document such as the national identity card led to the drafting of Law 1599/1986, which made it voluntary. The Church conducted a strong campaign then for the mandatory inclusion of religion. Its wishes were implemented with the change in government, and in 1991 a new law (1988/

1991) reintroduced mandatory inclusion of religion on each citizen's identity card (Dimitropoulos 2001: p. 152). Though voted in, neither of these laws was ever actually put into practice: Papadopoulos' original 1969 decree remained implemented by the Ministry of Public Order (which governs the police's issuance of the cards) throughout the debates in the 1980s and 1990s.

Also in 1991, the Convention of the Council of Europe drafted an article for the protection of the individual from the automated processing of information of personal nature.[22] The Convention article was further enforced by the European Parliament through the directive 95/46/EK (Papadopoulou 2000: p. 678). In order to conform to these European legislative developments, the Greek government passed Law 2472/1997, which lays out the "sensitive personal information" that the State should protect in the name of its citizens, including religious affiliation. According to this law, the use of such information by the State should be "relative to the aim" of its use (Dimitropoulos 2001: p. 153). The law also foresaw the establishment of the Hellenic Data Protection Authority, an independent authority charged with the protection of such sensitive information as religion.

A crisis in Church–State relations began in the spring of 2000 over the inclusion of religious affiliation on the national identity cards. The then Minister of Justice Mixalis Stathopoulos, appointed by the newly re-elected PASOK government, gave an interview in which he listed a number of religion-related legal reforms that he considered necessary, including the removal of religion from the national identity cards. His argument was that the government's continued inclusion of religion on the identity cards was in breach of Law 2472/1997. When the issue reached Constantinos Dafermos, President of the Hellenic Data Protection Authority, the Authority's council produced the judgment (on 15 May 2000) that religious belief is an aspect of "sensitive personal data" and should be excluded from national identity cards. A few days later, on 24 May 2000, the question was raised in parliament, and Prime Minister Simitis confirmed then that the government would implement the Data Protection Authority decision: information regarding citizens' religious identity would not appear on national identity cards printed in the future.

This issue came to dominate the national press for the remainder of 2000 and much of 2001. Most interesting was the political battle which ensued between Church and State. In a radio broadcast immediately following Stathopoulos' interview, Archbishop Christodoulos warned citizens that everyone, including the Prime Minister, should rally against the implementation of Stathopoulos' suggestion on the identity cards, for fear that other measures "against religion" would soon follow (such as the lessening of the role of religious education in schools, the removal of icons and crosses from public spaces, the canceling of the religious oath, and the requirement of civil, in additional to religious, marriage). Several hierarchs demanded that the government "take a stance" on Stathopoulos' statements, on the "cutting off of relations between Church and State" at the constitutional level, and on the inclusion of religious affiliation on the identity cards. One Metropolitan in particular characterized the whole issue as an "underhanded attack on Orthodoxy and Hellenism" (*Kathimerini* 9 May 2000: p. 1).

For the government's part, its then spokesman Dimitris Reppas initially declared that Stathopoulos had expressed "personal opinions" in the 8 May interview, but within days he stated that Minister Stathopoulos "does not act autonomously." This was interpreted by the press to mean that "[Stathopoulos] expressed the government perspective on the identity card issue" (*Eleutherotypia* 16 May 2000). Meanwhile, the Church's official stance was that at least voluntary inclusion of religion on one's identity card should be allowed (though its traditional position had been strictly for mandatory inclusion).[23] The Archbishop criticized the "progressives" who "fall on the Church like savage dogs," and called for a referendum on the matter.[24] The repeated argument for a national referendum was that "the minority cannot force its terms on the majority" (*Ethnos* 15 May 2000: p. 18). While the government was maintaining that "it does not intend to lead to a rift in Church–State relations," that "the issue of the identity cards consists of a practice of harmonization with European regulations and the protection of personal data," and that "in no case does [the government] wish to lessen the role of Orthodoxy," ecclesiastical officials were declaring that "Mr. Simitis, without realizing it, placed himself, the government, and his party within the ropes of the ring."[25]

Following the Prime Minister's statement in the parliament that the decision of the Data Protection Service on the matter would be implemented,[26] the Archbishop called for an extraordinary meeting of the Holy Synod for discussion of the Church's stance on the matter. Two demonstrations were planned, one to take place in Athens and the other in Thessaloniki, both in the month of June (*Kathimerini* 7 June 2000: p. 3; *To Vima* 7 June 2000: p. A7). Meanwhile, the Archbishop met with the President of the Republic, Constantine Stephanopoulos and requested the latter's intervention in the matter. Following the President's negative response to the Archbishop, indicating that the Constitution does not give him the right to intervene in institutional matters (*Kathimerini* 26 June 2000: p. 1), plans were made to take the case to the Council of State.[27] Finally, at the demonstrations, attended by thousands, the Archbishop announced that the Church would begin a collection of signatures in appeal for a referendum on the government identity card decision.[28] The aim, the Archbishop eventually announced, was to gather more signatures than the number of votes with which the Simitis government came to power in the previous elections.

Beyond the aforementioned European legislation and the government's own pronouncements, the most obvious indication of the "European dimension" of this issue is in the way in which certain actors within political and ecclesiastical circles portrayed the matter (or, perhaps more precisely, in the particular political and religious leaders' statements that the press chose to present). All throughout this Church–State struggle, "Europe" was presented, in a notably haphazard way, as a key figure in the equation. A few examples will suffice for our present purposes. Early on in the debate, Data Protection Authority president Constantinos Dafermos explained his personal opinion on the matter with reference to the fact that "in Europe they laugh at our identity cards with religion on them" (*Eleutherotypia* 13 May 2000). For his part, Christodoulos made the classic statement that "Europe may fill our pockets, but it can empty our souls" (*Kathimerini* 30 May 2000: p. 3). The main opposition party also picked up the cue, voiced here by the parliamentarian George Alogoskoufis: "... the question is to what extent as a country we will maintain certain religious, social and national traditions that we have, or if we will surrender every time, without any resistance, to the powers of the European Union" (*Eleutherotypia* 26 May 2000: p. 17). Meanwhile, foreign and English-language press reported the issue with headlines such as "Church Bashes Europe" (*The Hellenic Star* 1–7 June 2000). *The Observer* in particular noted that "... the Greek Orthodox Church is calling it a 'wild war', the Greek State a long overdue move to make all Hellenes 'more European',", thus prompting the reporter's own question: "Does Greece, the EU's only Orthodox nation, belong to the East or the West?"[29]

A more significant and little attended-to indication of the European/EU dimension of this issue is the most immediate precursor to the publicity surrounding it. Six months prior to the Stathopoulos interview, Foreign Minister George Papandreou had called for the formation of a committee to study issues of religious freedom. Among the subjects to be considered was the inclusion of religion on the national identity cards.[30] The reason for this action was the Foreign Minister's wish to address "the problems arising from the guilty verdicts against the country for violations of the European Treaty of Human Rights" and to discuss what legal measures should be taken to address the problem. Thus, seen as a matter of foreign affairs, the issue of the identity cards was placed within the framework of the Foreign Ministry's efforts to deal with matters that negatively affected Greece's place in Europe. When the Church was invited to participate and share its views on the issues under consideration, it showed "no will for dialog" (*Eleutherotypia* 26 May 2000: p. 17).

We now turn to the political implications of the Church's reaction. The Church did not manage to reverse the government's decision, and today Greek identity cards are printed without a slot for indicating one's religious beliefs. In spite of this fact, the Church's reaction still had significant effects in several areas of Greek political life. The political implications of the Church's involvement in the identity card issue may be divided into three interrelated domains: domestic policy, Church–State relations, and Greek–EU relations. I address each below, often with reference to the perspectives of Greek bureaucrats, politicians, constitutional specialists, sociologists, and political scientists whom I interviewed for this study.

In terms of domestic politics, a first notable factor is the number of signatures collected by the Church in its petition for a referendum on the issue. The fact that the Archbishop declared the Church's intent to collect more signatures than the number of votes which the ruling party won in the previous national elections is a clear signal of its involvement in politics. Moreover, the fact that it succeeded in this intent, by gathering over three million, is indicative of the Church's potential influence. As one bureaucrat indicates, the political power of this number cannot be overlooked: "It would not be wise for any politician to go into elections against the Archbishop." As a member of the Simitis government, he admits that many of the party's parliamentarians were disappointed with Simitis' decision, because with it they could expect to lose much of their local support. A Greek Member of the European Parliament (MEP) also emphasizes that the Church's influence over the electorate significantly affects many politicians' stances on issues even remotely related to the Church, because of their fear of the consequences in terms of electoral support.

Further evidence of the effect of the Church on domestic politics is the very intense way in which the identity card issue became a main platform of the conservative opposition party, the New Democracy. Its leader, Constantinos Karamanlis, was one of the first to sign the petition for a referendum, thus emphasizing the traditional close ties between the party and the Church. The party's manipulation of the issue for electoral purposes was so obvious that the press began ridiculing it as the "New Theocracy."

The influence of the Church in domestic politics became even more explicit in the municipal elections of October 2002. Although by that point the Church-run petition had been completed without having affected the government's decision, the Archbishop repeatedly declared that the issue was not closed. Rather, the municipal elections served as one more opportunity for confrontation with the government, when the Archbishop openly supported (through a widely televised sermon) a candidate for Mayor of Athens who had publicly backed the Church's view on the identity cards; at the same time, the hierarch was expressing indirect criticism against the New Democracy candidate in that same race, who was one of the very few in that party publicly to oppose the Church's stance. The candidate who enjoyed the Church's support, though without a base in an established political party and with no strong political platform, shocked politicians, journalists, and the Greek public in general by receiving a substantial percentage of the vote in the ensuing elections.[31] Furthermore, the widely publicized visits to the Archbishop by a number of candidates seeking his blessing, prior to the elections and in the wake of his aforementioned sermon, could be interpreted as nothing but the recognition of the Church's strong influence over domestic politics. Finally, even the fact that Foreign Minister George Papandreou henceforth made a point of personally informing the Archbishop (or, one might say, consulting him, depending on the perspective taken) on significant government policies, such as that on the United Nations proposal for solution to the Cyprus issue, was considered by many to be a direct effect of "lessons learned" by the government during the confrontation over identity cards.

In terms of the implications of the identity card issue on Church–State relations, many Greek bureaucrats and politicians note with regret that the numerous aspects of Church–State relations which urgently require revision were necessarily shelved in the aftermath of this conflict. "The Church," one bureaucrat declared, "is in a state of *self-defence* following the identity card issue. Any slightly religion-related issues addressed by the government are viewed with intense suspicion: they're afraid that we're preparing something against them." In the short run, according to many, the Church was the winner of this conflict with the State. Minister of Justice Stathopoulos was replaced in the subsequent government reshuffle, and his replacement enjoyed notably better relations with the Church hierarchy. Meanwhile, in a widely publicized interview, Prime Minister Simitis pointedly declared that the government had no more plans for policies related to the Church: a declaration which received little criticism from the press and the public.

However, in terms of long-term effects on Church–State relations, it must not be underestimated that the government did not back down on this particular policy, in spite of the extreme opposition it faced from the Church. This fact sets an important precedent; for, indeed, in all previous intense conflicts between Church and State in the history of modern Greece, significant concessions on particular policies were always made by the State. Finally, as one scholar notes, "… the Church reaction on this issue probably hurt the Church: it will not be able to easily mobilize people again, as the public understood that it was a wasted effort."

In terms of the impact of the "identity card crisis" on Greek–EU relations, an oft-cited effect is that it served to "blacken the image" of Greece within the EU. As one Greek MEP notes, the whole issue was far too reminiscent of the reactionary tactics of the Church during the crisis over the naming of Macedonia in the early 1990s. Much more consequential, though, are the effects related to the above-mentioned domains of domestic politics and Church–State relations. First, the identity card issue illustrates a special vulnerability in the Greek political system to the influences of the Church. When, under the threat of electoral losses, we see politicians more attentive to opinions emanating from the Archbishopric than from Brussels, we are obliged to recognize the Church as a significant factor in national–EU relations. Of course, the politicians' own responsibility in this must be highlighted: rather than counteract the Church's successful utilization of the national sensitivities of the Greek population by emphasizing the virtues of political and social equality, most politicians either fell silent or fed the intra- and inter-party conflict that arose under the identity card issue.

Second, the identity card issue illustrates a problematic intersection between Church–State and Greek–EU relations. There remain pending several governmental reforms which are either necessary for conformity with EU standards or have been explicitly demanded by the European Court of Human Rights, but which press on the sensitivities of the Church. For instance, enhanced provision of freedom of conscience by changing the nature of the mandatory religious education courses; guaranteed freedom of practice by removing the difficult barriers to the building of mosques or Protestant churches in Greece; simplification of the process through which conscientious objectors (who are mainly Jehovah's Witnesses) may be placed in social rather than military service;[32] and legislation allowing for cremation as an alternative to religious burial.[33] These are but a few examples of reforms which the Church of Greece has staunchly resisted. In light of the difficulty the government faced in implementing the identity card reform, we can expect significant delays in the implementation of such related measures.

Conclusion

In the wake of the identity card issue, it will be difficult for the Church to mobilize the people on similar issues again. Further reforms will likely be delayed, but carefully measured and consistent efforts on the part of the State should limit the opportunities for "Europe-bashing" on the part of the Church. Meanwhile, the recent enlargement of the EU entails a significantly larger Eastern Orthodox presence within the Union. This means two things: the Greek Church will feel less a threatened minority, and, as it increasingly identifies itself with the interests of other Orthodox populations, in the context of the EU, it will be less likely to play on specifically Greek nationalistic sensitivities. Finally, the Greek Orthodox Church is not a monolith. This much was clear in the division amongst the hierarchs over the identity card issue, with a number of clerics refraining from participation in the demonstrations and signature collection, and some even publicly criticizing the Archbishop's tactics. All of the above indicate that perhaps new links between religion, nation, and European norms can be expected in the future.

Notes

1   Evangelos Theodorou, *The Church of Greece*, 1959, p. 13; cited in Rexine (1972: p. 203).
2   This is the theme that runs through the works of Roudometof, Manitakis, Dimitropoulos, Anagnostopoulou, and many others.
3   Nikos Kokosalakis (1987: pp. 223–42, citation from pp. 230–1). He also notes that more than 6,000 priests and a large number of bishops were killed during the revolution, including Patriarch Gregorious V.
4   The layman's presence was required for the drafting of Synodal decisions, which were then subject to government approval (Dimitropoulos 2001: p. 59).
5   Not least in the hope that this would also entail an enhancement of their wages. See Kokosalakis (1987: p. 239).
6   Dimitropoulos (2001: p. 62). In ecclesiastical terms, this meant that the Greek Orthodox Church was in communion with the other Orthodox churches, and that matters relating to dogma or faith must be referred to the Patriarchate. See also Rexine (1972: pp. 204–5).
7   The research for Kent's dissertation began during the time of the military dictatorship; to date, it is amongst relatively few sources providing detailed insight into a period of Greek history which is still under-represented in the literature.

8 The regime issued a decree which demanded that films be compatible with "the religious beliefs and traditions of the Greek people, as well as with public order and national security" (Kent 1971: p. 400).

9 Kent also provides interesting insight into the personal backgrounds of each of the three main junta leaders. This helps us understand, beyond reasons of political expedience and the need to legitimate their rule, the extent to which the colonels' attachment to religion and conservatism also had to do with their own backgrounds. Each was from a conservative village or small town in rural Greece, and each had also suffered family losses during the civil war.

10 Of course, the ECHR, founded by the European Treaty of Human Rights, is officially linked to the Council of Europe, and not directly to the EU. However, there is no question that the ECHR record of individual countries is especially important to the EU.

11 "The Europe of spiritual values and the role of the Greek Orthodox and of Education," addressed to a crowd of teachers at the National Theatre, 21 January 1999.

12 Cited in Nikos Alivizatos (1999: p. 23).

13 See Papastathis (1995: p. 86). The State provides the salaries of prelates; priests who serve in a parish; deacons; preachers; and laymen employed by the Church. These persons also receive pensions from the State when retired. As Papastathis notes, the State also receives 35 percent of all parish revenues. Certain tax exemptions apply to other faiths as well.

14 We shall expand on this subject in reference to the national identity card issue. For further discussion of this theme, see Kokosalakis (1995: pp. 253–6). See also Vassiliki Georgiadou (1995: pp. 295–315). See in particular her discussion (p. 308) of the fluctuating relationship between the Church and the PASOK government of 1981-7. As Kokosalakis (1987: p. 232) notes, in its electoral manifesto before the 1981 elections, PASOK both proposed the "administrative separation" of Church and State, and stated that "the bonds of the Church with the nation (to ethnos) must be preserved."

15 The application must be signed by 50 families residing in the area. The local bishop is to forward his opinion to the Minister of Education and Religious Affairs on the "necessity" of such a building. The law states that, for the license, there must be a real need for worship which cannot be satisfied due to the lack of other churches/houses of worship of the same faith in the geographical area.

16 See Dimitropoulos (2001: pp. 134–5) for details of individual cases.

17 Law 1672/1939. See Alivizatos (1999: p. 30) for the full operative definition of proselytism (the quotation given here is only part of the definition) and for an analysis of its problematic aspects.

18 Alivizatos (1999) also notes, however, that the ECHR missed an opportunity to change this state of affairs through its ruling on the Kokkinakis case. It condemned Greece for unmotivated enforcement of the anti-proselytism provision, but ruled that member states have a legitimate interest to prosecute "improper proselytism," without giving its own definition of this term.

19 This according to Law 1566/1985.

20 This is a matter of open debate. The StE (*Symbouleio tis Epikrateias*, i.e. the Council of State, which is the highest national court, equivalent to the "Supreme Court") has issued an "opinion" that the religion courses should have a *thriskeiologiko* (of the science of religion), not catechetical, character: an opinion which, of course, has received great criticism from the Church. Furthermore, both the StE and the Data Protection Authority have recently expressed the opinion that the current process by which one may be exempted from the course (requiring proclamation of another faith) should also be amended. Finally, in the author's opinion, the current character

of the religion courses is also in conflict with the operative laws against proselytism (i.e. under the aforementioned loose definition of the term, the religion courses in public schools could also be interpreted as proselytism).

21 Now a non-Orthodox may be appointed as teacher in a primary school with at least two teaching positions, in which case the religion course is taught by his/her Orthodox colleague. The latter fact effectively means that non-Orthodox teachers still may not be hired at schools with positions for only one teacher. At the time of writing, this issue was under discussion at the StE, which issued its opinion that non-Orthodox teachers should be allowed to teach even the course on religion.

22 This translated into Greek legislation as Law 2068/1991. See Lina Papadopoulou (2000: pp. 675–723, note from p. 678).

23 The Holy Synod was quite divided on the issue. See *Ta Nea* (26 May 2000: p. 9).

24 He declared: "We will not become gravediggers of our ethnos. We are more than they who want to destroy the country. The People endorse what I say. Let there then be a referendum." *To Vima* (15 May 2000: p. A3).

25 *Kathimerini* (26 May 2000: p. 5). Father Eustathios Kollas, President of the Clergy, stated further, "… the Holy Synod does not care if religion is legally written on the identity cards or not, because either way it will be written, and with capital letters. I am considering proposing that citizens precede their signatures with the capital letters XO [i.e. Orthodox Christian]."

26 The issue was raised while Maria Damanaki of the *Synaspismo* Party questioned the Prime Minister. Simitis responded, "The inclusion of religion on the identity cards limits and offends the independence of the citizen. The citizen can and should be free to believe and not reveal what he/she believes. Therefore the inclusion of religion … can neither be required nor voluntary." See *Kathimerini* (25 May 2000: p. 5).

27 See *To Vima* (25 May 2000: p. A.7) and *Kathimerini* (23 August 2000) for information on the planning of the case, which reached the court on 1 December 2000. The case was actually taken to the StE by a group called the "Orthodox Movement of Constitutional Legality," but for most observers it was clear that this group acted on behalf of the Church. The court decided by majority that both the voluntary and mandatory inclusion of religion on the national identity cards are in antithesis with Article 13, Paragraph 1 of the Constitution, in which freedom of religious conscience is set out. For a thorough analysis of the StE decision, see Dimitropoulos (2001: pp. 154–7).

28 Police estimated 100,000 demonstrators at the 21 June demonstration in Athens; the Church estimated over 500,000.

29 "Greek Church stirs holy war over ID cards," *The Observer* (28 May 2000).

30 Other issues to be discussed were proselytism, conscientious objection, and religious education in schools: all of which have led to complaints against the Greek state by citizens of minority faiths.

31 Georgios Karatzaferis, the candidate supported by the Archbishop, who declared in a widely publicized sermon during Sunday liturgy that those who would vote for Karatzaferis were "good Christians," received 12 percent of the vote, while the New Democracy candidate, Ioannis Tzannetakos, received only 2 percent.

32 Many of the cases against the Greek state in the ECHR are related to conscientious objection. Beyond the challenges non-Orthodox citizens face in gaining the right to alternative service, they sometimes face further problems when assigned to Church-run welfare services.

33 Tabatha Morgan, "Crematoria plan outrages Greek Church," report on the Church's resistance to legislation providing for the practice of cremation in Greece. BBC Europe, 11 April 2002.

4 Passage to Turkishness
Immigration and religion in modern Turkey

Soner Cagaptay

The use of the term "Turk" in modern Turkey is a puzzling phenomenon. Most people in the country see all Muslims as Turks, regardless of their ethnicity or language. In view of this, not only ethnic Turks, but also other Muslims such as Kurds, Circassians, or Bosnians are regarded as Turks, while non-Muslims, especially Christians (including Armenians and Greeks) are not, even when they speak Turkish. This is not simply a matter of semantics: in Turkey, being a Turk has tangible benefits. Since only Turks are full members of the nation and considered to be loyal citizens, this perception is key to joining the mainstream of the country.

An analysis of Turkish nationalism would help understand this complex relationship between religion and nationality. Turkish nationalism materialized during the last decades of the Ottoman Empire. However, it was after Mustafa Kemal Atatürk and his cadres established the Turkish Republic in 1923 that nationalism rose to prominence in Turkey. With the emergence and consolidation of the Kemalist state in the 1920s and the 1930s, nationalism became one leg of the ideological tripod of young Turkey, together with secularism and Westernization. A specific understanding of what constitutes Turkishness became legally enforced and publicly accepted in this era. The 1920s and the 1930s were a decade of authoritarian nationalisms all over eastern Europe, including Turkey.[1]

Since the 1930s, Ankara's understanding of what constitutes Turkishness, enforced through many state practices in this decade, has dominated the relations between Ankara and its citizens, especially the non-Muslim and non-Turkish groups. Hence, a study of nationalism in Turkey in the inter-war period with an emphasis on the relations between the state and the minorities seems useful to understand the aforementioned nationality-related dilemmas of contemporary Turkey. Nationalism of the Kemalist era juxtaposed territory, religion, and ethnicity, producing a rather complex definition of Turkishness. In an attempt to define this phenomenon in contemporary Turkey, I will focus on the largely ignored immigration and population resettlement policies of the inter-war Kemalist state.[2]

Turkey (Anatolia and Thrace) had been part of the vast multi-ethnic Ottoman Empire. Muslims and Christians coexisted in Turkey. As late as 1912, Christians made up 20 percent of Turkey's population; fifteen years later, in 1927, they had dropped to as few as 2.64 percent (McCarthy 1982: pp. 60–8; *Istatistik Yilligi* 1929: p. 45, 1934–5: p. 159). Another demographic change was brought about by an influx of Muslim immigrants. Throughout the dissolution of the Ottoman Empire, many Ottoman Muslims, including Turks, but also Bosnian, Greek, Serbian, Macedonian, Albanian, and Bulgarian Muslims (Pomaks), who faced extermination or repression in the newly independent Balkan states, fled to Anatolia. In addition, Turks, Circassians, and others arrived in Anatolia from the Black Sea basin. (These people had been fleeing Russian expansionism in southern Russia, the Crimea and the Caucasus since the late eighteenth century.)[3] The immigrants joined Turkey's autochthonous Muslim groups of Turks, Kurds, Arabs, Georgians, and Lazes, and added to Anatolia's Muslim and Turkish demographic base, diluting the demographic weight of the Christians (Ahmad 1969: pp. 152–3; McCarthy 1995: p. 336). Because of these population shifts, by the 1920s, Turkey had become home to a largely Turkish, yet multi-ethnic, Muslim majority.[4] In this population, the Kurds were the most significant non-Turkish nationality. Hence, as a nation-state, Kemalist Turkey was bound to deal with the country's lingering heterogeneity.

During the 1920s, with secularism as its cornerstone, Kemalism turned its back on both Islam and irredentism, and promoted a territorial definition of the Turkish nation (Inan 1969: p. 364; Karpat 1991: p. 50).[5] An emphasis on Turkey (Anatolia and Thrace) became a pronounced tendency within Turkish nationalism. Article 88 of the Turkish Constitution of 1924 stipulated: "The People of Turkey, regardless of religion and race, are Turks as regards Turkish citizenship."[6] Atatürk declared: "The people of Turkey, who have established the Turkish state, are called the Turkish nation" (Inan 1969: p. 351). He emphasized a shared past and body of interests and the desire to live together as the common denominators of the nation (ibid.: p. 379). The official definition of the Turkish nation focused on a voluntaristic linguistic–territorial formula. Accordingly, for instance, Article 5 of the 1927 by-laws of Turkey's ruling Republican People's Party stipulated that "the Party was convinced that the strongest link among the

citizens was unity in language, unity in feelings and unity in ideas."[7]
Moreover, Article 88 of the Turkish Constitution dictated that persons
"granted Turkish citizenship by law, are Turks."[8] This is where the
immigrant non-Turkish Muslims came in. The Kemalists thought it
feasible and desirable to assimilate them into the Turkish nation. In
fact, Islam had already been an avenue towards Turkishness among
them. Being in Turkey had provided them with the conditions of
assimilability under the Turkish language and through the Muslim religion (Keyder 1997: p. 36).[9] Consequently, by the 1920s very few immigrant non-Turkish Muslims still spoke their former native languages.

The Kemalists expected that the autochthonous Muslims would
assimilate quickly as well. In a speech to the Turkish parliament in
1920, Mustafa Kemal said: "You, the members of this exalted Assembly, are not just Turks, or Circassians, or Kurds, or Lazes; you are composed of all the Islamic elements and constitute a coherent whole."[10]
Yet, the local Muslims did not have the same incentives as the immigrant Muslims to merge into the Turkish nation. They had been neither
uprooted from their homelands nor bereft of their cultural and social
structures due to expulsion. Additionally, they lived in compact territo-
ries. Among them, the Kurds were the majority in large parts of south-
eastern Turkey.[11] Of all the Muslim groups, they were the least likely to
assimilate.

The 1930s and the "Turkish History Thesis"

The emergence of the "Turkish History Thesis" in 1931 marked the
ascendancy of Turkish nationalism.[12] According to this thesis, as
stressed in one of the seminal works of this period, *Türk Tarihinin Ana
Hatlarina Methal* [Introduction to the General Themes of Turkish
History] (1930: pp. 50–8), put together by the "Members of the Society
for the Study of Turkish History," the Turks were a great and ancient
race. The work claimed that, thousands of years ago, the Turks had
lived in Central Asia, where they had created a bright civilization
around an inner sea. When this inner sea had dried up due to climatic
changes, they had left Central Asia, and moved in all directions to civi-
lize the rest of the world, including Anatolia. Accordingly, Anatolia
was the Turkish homeland since the Turks had been its autochthonous
population (ibid.: p. 8).

Over time, the Turks had "crossed with other races"; however, the
Turkish language had preserved their memories, cultural characteristics, and everything else that made them a nation, including the Turks'
most cherished possession, the Turkish intellect (Inan 1969: p. 352;

Türk Tarihinin Ana Hatlarina Methal 1930: p. 38). Since the Turkish language had preserved the nation, one had to speak it to prove that one was of ethnic Turkish descent and thereby eligible for membership in the Turkish nation. This ethnicist definition of the nation-through-language placed the non-Turkish speakers of Turkey in a precarious position.

Yet the Kemalist regime did not view the non-Turks as an undifferentiated mass. It saw the Muslims and the non-Muslims differently. Lectures given by Recep (Peker) (1888–1950), Secretary General of the Republican People's Party and a prominent Kemalist ideologue, elaborated this view with a positive, albeit patronizing approach toward non-Muslims: "We need to voice our ideas on our Christian and Jewish citizens with equal clarity. Our party sees these citizens as full Turks, on condition that they participate in ... the unity in language and in ideals." (Peker 1931: p. 7) But Peker also inserted the caveat that even then non-Muslims would not be considered as ethnic Turks since "according to daily-progressing historical evidence, the matter of blood ties and historical links between us and these masses is beyond our contemporary debate" (ibid.: p. 6). In other words, not all Turkish citizens were members of the Turkish nation. With regard to the non-Turkish Muslims, however, Peker considered them as Turks: "We accept as our own those citizens in the contemporary Turkish political and social community, on whom ideas have been imposed that they are Kurds, Circassians and even Lazes and Pomaks. It is our duty to correct these false conceptions (among them) ... " (ibid.). As the Kemalists believed that the Kurds (and the other Muslim groups) did not need to foster a separate ethnic identity, a Turkish dictionary, published in this period, confirmed this attitude by describing the Kurds as an *"ahali* [population] living around the Iranian border" (Alaettin 1930: p. 638).

How did this position affect Turkey's ethnic and religious minorities? So far, I have focused on the ideology of Kemalist nationalism. However, a deeper analysis of Turkish nationalism requires one to look at the practices of the Kemalist state, including the relations between Ankara and the minorities. Here, I will focus on one aspect of this relationship, namely policies toward immigration and population resettlement. This will help us develop a better understanding of contemporary Turkish nationalism as shaped by inter-war Kemalism.

Immigration to Turkey during the early republican era

Throughout the 1920s and the 1930s, Turks and Muslims from various parts of the former Ottoman Empire came to the country that they began to consider home. Immigrants, mainly from the Balkans, but also from the Aegean islands, Cyprus, Hatay (the Sancak of Alexandratta), the Middle East, and the Soviet Union poured into Turkey. The bulk of the immigrants were Balkan Turks and Muslims, who faced harassment and discrimination in their homelands and opted for Turkey's comfort and the attraction of a new nation. The drawing power of the new Turkey was so strong that Turkish immigrants arrived from as far as Yemen, Trans-Jordan, and Finland.[13] According to one estimate, between 1921 and 1939, 719,808 people entered Turkey as immigrants (*Istatistik Yilligi* 1929: p. 65, 1938–9: p. 89). Another calculation puts the number of immigrants from 1923 through 1938 at 801,818 (Kazgan 1983: p. 1556). In any case, this was a sizable influx, given that in 1927 the country's population was 13,542,795.

An analysis of Turkey's immigration policies in this period reveals that, despite its rhetoric of linguistic and even civic-voluntaristic definitions of nationhood, in practice Kemalism saw Turkishness as a derivative of religion. In other words, all Muslim rump of the Ottoman Empire (except the Arabs) who were in Turkey or who came to Turkey were seen as Turks, even if they were not ethnic Turks. During this era, Turkey signed treaties with Greece and Romania to facilitate emigration from these countries. The government also entered accords with Albania, Armenia, and Bulgaria to regulate its affairs with them. Interestingly, these treaties mentioned not the Turks, but the Muslims as the primary object of Turkey's interest.[14]

Notwithstanding their belief in the ethnic definition of the nation, the Kemalists were aware of Islam's role in nation-building in Turkey, especially, vis-à-vis the non-Turkish Balkan Muslims. Like the Turks, the Balkan Muslims descended from the Turkish-Muslim ethnos of the Ottoman Empire. Moreover, compared to the Anatolian Muslims, these people were better educated and more prosperous. Because Turkey was an under-populated and devastated country in the 1920s, Ankara desperately needed the human capital of these Muslims. Thus, for ideological, demographic, and economic reasons, the Kemalists opened the country's doors to the Muslim immigrants from the Balkans. Ankara actively promoted Muslim immigration from the Balkans.[15]

In addition to the Balkan immigrants, Turks of Cyprus, Hatay, Iraq, Iran, and the Soviet Union also came to the country. These people opted for Turkey so that they could live in a Turkish state, while at least the Caucasus Turks immigrated also in order to escape Soviet communism. A British report from 1928 recorded the diversity of the immigrants:

They [the Kemalists] advertise the desire of the Cypriots, Syrians and other Muslim inhabitants from the Dodecanese Caucasus and elsewhere to settle in Turkey. The press states that land and houses made vacant by the departure of the Greek elements are being apportioned to Cypriots in the Smyrna neighborhood; that land in north-eastern Turkey is being prepared for a large influx of Moslems from the Caucasus; and that eastern Turkey is being populated by emigrants from Yugoslavia, Bulgaria and Greece in considerable numbers.[16]

The resettlement law of 1926

As the Ottoman Turkish-Muslims poured into the country, Turkey needed legislation to cope with the influx. The first resettlement law, *Iskan Kanunu* (Nr. 885), was adopted on 31 May 1926. This law began with a definition of how one could qualify as an immigrant, stating in its second article: "Those people who do not share the Turkish *hars* [culture] ... will not be admitted as immigrants."[17]

During the deliberations on this law, the members of the Turkish parliament agreed that Turkish *hars* would be the basis of future immigration to Turkey.[18] Ziya Gökalp, one of the founding fathers of Turkish nationalism, inspired the Kemalists in their usage of the word *hars*. According to Gökalp (1952: p. 15), the nation was a community of individuals united by a shared *hars*, and based on common education, morality, socialization, and aesthetics. Gökalp downplayed ethnicity and defined the nation through collective values. Hence, in the Resettlement Law, the word *hars* referred to Islam and the Turkish language, as well as to the common past and future and to the values of the Ottoman Turkish-Muslims.

This law facilitated the immigration of Turkish and Muslim ex-Ottomans into Turkey. Simultaneously, it prohibited non-Muslim ex-Ottomans from immigrating. In demonstration of this, on 19 January 1929, the Directorate General for Resettlement (*Iskan Umum Müdüriyeti* [IUM]) asked that Greeks coming from various places not be admitted as refugees since their "resettlement and maintenance is not possible" due to "economic hardships" (BCA 272.11/ 15.54.7. 19 January 1929). While Turkey admitted non-Turkish Muslims, the government used its resettlement policies to enhance the Turkish character of the population. For instance, on 15 October 1925, the IUM decided that the Maras province "whose inhabitants were of various elements, needed Turkish immigrants" (BCA 272.11/46.79.19. 15 October 1925). In another example, on 26 December 1926, the IUM asked that Turkish immigrants coming from Russia be "resettled in Van and the nearby villages on the Van plain," a heavily Kurdish area of the country (BCA 272.11/22.113.28. 26 December 1926).

Additionally, the government took care to distinguish the non-Turkish immigrants from the Turkish ones. During the Turk–Greek population exchange, for instance, it seemed likely that the Muslim Chamuria (Akarnania) Albanians, who lived in the Greek Epirus, would be sent to Turkey. The government was anxious about a flow of Albanians into Turkey, and inquired to see if this group was going to be considered exchangeable (BCA 030.18.1.2/11.43.18. 14 September 1924). Some of these Muslims declared to the mixed-exchange commission in Parga, Epirus, that they were Turks. Hence, they were allowed into the exchange by the commission (BCA 030.18.1.2/12.65.5. 28 December 1924). Ankara was anxious to find out if these individuals were ethnic Turks (BCA 272.11/20.99.4. 9 November 1924). In the end, some Chamuria Albanians immigrated to Turkey, following which the Turkish government facilitated their departure for third countries. On 6 May 1925, Ankara issued a decree stipulating that "240 people of the Albanian race, who had come from Greece with the population exchange, could leave for abroad" (BCA 030.18.1.2/13.30.9. 6 May 1925).

Resettlement policies toward the Kurds in the 1920s

As it aimed to facilitate the country's repopulation and its Turkification, the Resettlement Law also focused on domestic population issues. Accordingly, it authorized the Ministry of Interior "to relocate the nomadic tribes and others around suitable centers."[17] (The term "nomad" in the republican jargon was a euphemism for the Kurds, and the occasional Roma, the only migrant groups in Turkey by the late 1920s). Consequently, this clause opened the way for the gradual assimilation of the Kurds by turning them into settled people, allowing the government to uproot them from their homelands and resettle them elsewhere among the Turks.[19] In noting this, Tevfik Rüstü Aras (1883–1972), the Turkish Minister of Foreign Affairs, told the British Ambassador Sir George R. Clerk (1874–1951) in 1926, perhaps with some exaggeration, that "the Turkish Government was determined to clear out the Kurds from their valleys, the richest part of Turkey today, and to settle Turkish peasants there." These Kurds would be resettled among the Turks.

Despite the legal framework provided by the Resettlement Law of 1926, however, the resettlement of the Kurds did not become a widespread policy during the 1920s. One reason for this may have been that Turkey's view toward the Kurdish question gave priority to security, that is control of the Kurdish population. Turkey regarded colonization of the East and resettlement of the Kurds as secondary, future goals. In 1930, Aras told the British representative to the League of Nations in Geneva:

> For the moment, the Turkish Government's Kurdish policy consists of military occupation for the purpose of maintaining order and the complete and absolute disarmament of the population. It is possible to envisage in the future an intense colonization so that the Kurds may be drowned in the huge mass of the Turkish population.[20]

Accordingly, the Kurds moved to western Turkey between 1920 and 1932 were a mere 2,774 out of the 742,720 people who were resettled in the country during that period. Of this sum, 499,239 were exchangees, covered by the Turk–Greek population exchange treaty, and 172,029 were non-exchangees (i.e. Muslim immigrants from Greece and other neighboring countries, who were not covered by the population exchange treaty). In addition, 14,312 people resettled during this period were *harikzede* (i.e. those made homeless by fire) who had lost their homes due to wartime destruction, especially the burning of towns by the Russian, Greek, and Armenian forces between World War I and the Turkish Independence War. An additional 35,936 people in the resettled population were refugees, while 18,430 people were classified as *yerli ahali* (native populace).[21]

Turkey resorted to forced relocation of the Kurds during the 1920s mostly to pacify the insurgent elements. For instance, following an uprising in the Agri region in 1927, the government passed Law Nr. 1097, which decreed the relocation of "about fourteen hundred individuals from Agri province and the Eastern martial law area to the Western provinces."[22] Although free "to travel around the Western provinces," they were not to return to the east. In another case of limited resettlement, on 20 November 1927, the government moved 41 people, who lived in ten households in Bitlis province, to western Turkey (BCA 272.11/23.120.18. 20 November 1927). There was compulsory relocation of the Kurds, as well, in the aftermath of the abortive Agri uprising of 1930. At that time, the government was reported to be planning to replace the Kurds in this area with Turks. In July 1930, Aras told British Ambassador Clerk that, after the rebellion, "it would be necessary to re-people the whole district with Turkish refugees from elsewhere."[23]

Leadership of Kurdish nationalists, such as the members of leading families, was subjected to relocation, too. In particular, those people who were implicated in anti-government uprisings were moved to western Turkey. A British traveler to eastern Turkey noted in 1929 that, because of such policies, "there is not, I was told, a single wealthy or powerful Kurd in Turkish Kurdistan today."[24]

In the 1920s, in addition to the Kurds, other groups such as the Armenians also were subjected to limited resettlement. For instance, a letter written from the governor of Aksaray on 31 August 1928 asked for permission from the Ministry of Interior to relocate three Armenians from Mardin, who had been resettled in the Arapsun district of Aksaray. According to the letter, these Armenians, "Atabel, son of Sahin; Kirkor, son of Yorki; and Ohannis, son of Kevork," had been unable to make a living in Arapsun and were in financial despair. The governor asked if the three men could be relocated to Aksaray, where he expected that they could engage in trade and make a living (BCA 272.12/62.185.1. 31 August 1929).

Given the limited nature of the Kurds' relocation, much of the ambition vis-à-vis its potential remained on paper or in rumors. For instance, a 1928 scheme by the Turkish government to import 60,000 Muslims from the Caucasus for settlement among the Kurds[25] never took place. On the other hand, in 1930, American diplomatic sources reported that a rumor had come their way that "the Turkish authorities plan to exterminate the Kurds and to repopulate Turkish Kurdistan with Turks now resident in Soviet Russia, notably in Azerbaijan, where they are numerous."[26] Such a plan, of course, did not materialize. Nevertheless, such rumors had the "effect of causing a great deal of disquietude amongst the thousands of the inhabitants to whom such a law would be applicable."[27]

The resettlement of the Kurds in the 1930s

Despite its low-level application in the 1920s, the idea of assimilating the Kurds through relocation survived beyond that decade into the 1930s, when Turkishness came to be defined by means of ethnicity and population engineering in the service of Turkish nationalism emerged as a valuable concept. A new Resettlement Law (Nr. 2520), which was passed on 13 June 1934, demonstrated this development.[28] During the discussions of this law in the Turkish parliament, MP Mustafa Nasit Hakki (Ulug) (1902–77) (Kütahya) emphasized the ethnicist nature of this new legislation: "The Resettlement Law is distinguished as one of the foremost laws of the revolution since it will steep all who live in this land with the honor and the appreciation of being Turkish."[29]

The first article of the new Resettlement Law stated: "The Ministry of Interior is assigned the powers to correct ... the distribution and locale of the population in Turkey in accordance with affiliation to Turkish culture."[30] The legislation also designated three zones in Turkey for the implementation of this policy. They were: Zone 1, set aside for "populations who share the Turkish culture"; Zone 2, for the "... relocation and resettlement of populations which are to be assimilated into the Turkish culture"; and Zone 3, areas to be vacated and closed to resettlement and habitation due to "sanitary, economic, cultural, political, military and security" reasons.[31]

People who lived in Zone 1 areas and were of Turkish origin, but had forgotten Turkish, were to be resettled in villages, towns, and cities in Zone 1, "whose population shared the Turkish culture." Tribal or nomadic people, as well as individuals "who did not share the Turkish culture" would not be allowed to settle in or enter Zone 1, even if they were original inhabitants of the area.[32] Tribal populations that lived in Zone 1 areas and that did not speak Turkish would be resettled in Zone 2 areas of the country, except in the following (Zone 1) districts:

- "Areas in which resettlement is forbidden or limited in accordance with the decision of the Cabinet of Ministers."
- "Those parts of the First, Third and Fourth Inspectorates that are set aside for the resettlement of Turkish immigrants from foreign countries."[33]
- Areas in Diyarbakir, Siirt, Van, Bitlis, Sivas, Erzincan, Erzurum, Malatya, Mardin, Urfa, Bingol, Agri, Igdir, Tunceli, Gümüshane, Maras, and Gaziantep, such as a "twenty kilometer belt on both sides of railway lines, radial sectors centered around urban zones, planes, mining zones and regions, lake Van basin," border zones, river valleys, as well as the Igdir, Erzincan, Elbistan, and Malatya planes.[34]

The focus of these stipulations was the Kurds, whom the laws in the 1920s and the 1930s described in varying ways, including "tribal populations that do not speak Turkish,"[34] or "people who do not share the Turkish culture."[35] For instance, a 1939 amendment to the Resettlement Law stated in reference to the Kurds that "people who are not of Turkish origin and who do not share the Turkish culture" were banned from resettling in Zone 1.[36]

The government planned to resettle the Turks in Zone 1 areas, from which the Kurds were banned. This would enable Ankara to carve an axis of Turkishness into the Kurdish heartland in the east.[37] In this endeavor, Ankara gave priority to Turks from the eastern Black Sea littoral, the most densely populated area of the country.[38] A report entitled *Sark Islahat Raporu* [Report on Reform in the East] and dated September 1925 had suggested this.[39] This report had given the inhabitants of Trabzon and Rize provinces the right of way for resettlement in the Murat river valley as well as in the Lake Van basin (Bayrak 1993: p. 483). In accordance with this, for instance, on 5 November 1933, Ankara decided to resettle "9,836 landless peasants from Trabzon and Çoruh *vilayets* around lake Van," a Zone 2 area in which Kurdish settlement had been prohibited (BCA 030.18.1.2/40.77.9. 5 November 1933).

The next stage of the plan was that the Kurds would be resettled in Zone 2 areas, where they would mix with the Turks. Article 9 of the Resettlement Law stated: "The Ministry of Interior is entitled to ... resettle migrant Roma and nomads, who do not share the Turkish culture, by spreading them around to Turkish towns and villages."[40] Besides, the Ministry was authorized to "distribute tribal members, who were Turkish subjects and who did not belong to Turkish culture, to Zone 2."[41] The Kemalists thought that, since the Turks and the Kurds shared a common religious identity, they could assimilate the Kurds by integrating them with the Turks. Hence, the Resettlement Law stipulated that those people who were resettled had to stay a minimum of ten years in their new homes.[42]

If, however, these policies failed, and should the Kurds prove to be troublesome, the Ministry of Interior was empowered to "... deport nomads, who do not share the Turkish culture, outside the national boundaries." Pursuant to this, the law dictated the following:

> The Ministry of Interior is entitled to take the necessary cultural, military, political, social, and security measures against those people who share the Turkish culture but speak a language other than Turkish, or against those people who do not share the Turkish culture. These measures, not to be applied collectively, include resettlement and denaturalization.[43]

The government did resort to the resettlement of the Kurds during the 1930s. In accordance with this, in 1932, security forces stormed various areas of unrest and deported the Kurdish inhabitants of these regions to the Turkish provinces in western Turkey.[44] Even then, however, the resettlement of the Kurds in western Turkey did not turn into a massive project. The total number of Kurds relocated to western Turkey in the 1930s was 25,381 people in 5,074 households.[45]

Race and ethnicity in the resettlement policies of the 1930s

Concomitant with the "Turkish History Thesis," race and ethnicity became important concepts in Turkish resettlement policies, especially in the Resettlement Law of 1934, as demonstrated by Article 7 of this legislation. This clause, which dealt with aid to the immigrants, stipulated that "immigrants who belong to the Turkish *soy* [race, origin] might settle wherever they wish, so long as they have not applied for material help from the government." However, "immigrants who do not belong to the Turkish race" had to settle where the government had asked them to, whether or not they had requested aid from the government.[46]

During the discussion of this law in the Turkish parliament, Sükrü Kaya (1883–1959), the Minister of Interior Affairs, said that the term *soy* in this legislation meant "race."[47] This word was used often in the Kemalist laws and acts of the 1920s and 1930s. In this, the Kemalists referred to the conventional, nineteenth-century usage of this term, when race had been synonymous with nation. In the early twentieth century, Nazism and other racist ideologies transformed the term "race" by attaching modifiers drawn from biology, genetics, bloodline, and physical attributes.[48] However, in the Kemalist usage, the meaning of the word *soy* was closer to its nineteenth-century connotations than to those definitions of the twentieth century. Hence, when the word *soy* appeared very frequently in the Turkish documents during the 1930s, it referred to a national community rather than to a biological one. As indicated earlier, language was seen as a primary marker of Turkishness. True, in the minds of the Kemalists, *soy* was an immutable category, but it was about ethnicity and not about biology. By referring to race in the Resettlement Law, Kemalism took Turkish ethnicity as a central concept. In the minds of the republican cadres, Turkishness was not about religion or voluntaristic declarations, it was about language and ethnicity.

Immigration matrix

Nonetheless, despite its tilt towards race and ethnicity in resettlement and immigration matters, the Kemalist Turkish state allowed certain non-Turks to be immigrants. An article of the Resettlement Law provided that, "following approval by the Ministry of Interior, settled or nomadic individuals of Turkish origin and settled persons who share the Turkish culture" would qualify as immigrants.[49] A deductive reading of this clause reveals that it banned the immigration of (1) "settled persons who do not share the Turkish culture," and (2) "nomadic individuals of non-Turkish origin." On the other hand, the clause permitted the immigration of (1) "settled or nomadic individuals of Turkish origin" and (2) "settled persons who share the Turkish culture."

Based on Gökalp's definition, the term "Turkish culture" in this law referred to the common heritage of the Ottoman-Turkish Muslims. It covered their joint history, traditions, belief system, values, and mores. Accordingly, the phrase "settled persons who do not share the Turkish culture" apparently referred to the non-Muslims. A British diplomatic record elaborated on this interpretation: "It could be established that persons in Turkey of non-Turkish culture are the same as the non-Moslem minorities."[50] Consequently, the phrase "settled persons who do not share the Turkish culture" applied to the urban non-Muslims in Turkey's vicinity, including the Greeks, Bulgarians, and other Balkan Christians, as well as the Russians, Armenians, Georgians, and Jews.

On the other hand, the term "nomadic individual" in this law was a Kemalist euphemism for the Kurds and Roma in Turkey. When applied to potential immigrants in Turkey's vicinity, this phrase also would have covered the Arabs, Assyrians, Circassians, and other Muslims of the Caucasus, the major nomadic groups in Turkey's neighborhood in the 1930s. Hence, the Resettlement Law, which prevented "nomadic individuals of non-Turkish origin" from immigrating, blocked the Kurds, Roma, Arabs, Assyrians, Circassians, and other Muslims of the Caucasus from coming to Turkey.

The meaning of the phrase "settled or nomadic individuals of Turkish origin" in this clause is clear. This referred to ethnic Turks, including those people from the Balkans, Cyprus, and the Dodecanese Islands, as well as Azeris, Balkars, Karaçays, Karapapaks, Tatars, Turkmen, and other Turkic groups in the country's vicinity.

Finally, the phrase "settled persons who share the Turkish culture" needs elaboration. While the term "Turkish culture" referred to Ottoman-Turkish Muslims, this term covered the urban Ottoman-Turkish Muslims in Turkey's vicinity. Hence, as a Kemalist euphemism, the term "settled persons who share the Turkish culture" referred to the Balkan Muslims who were not Turks.

Muslims of the Balkans and Caucasus in the resettlement policies of the 1930s

Consequently, in addition to Turks from the Balkans, the Aegean, the Middle East, and the Caucasus, non-Turkish Balkan Muslims also were allowed to immigrate to Kemalist Turkey in the inter-war period. According to the Kemalists, this was part of the Ottoman legacy. Dr Refik Ibrahim Saydam (1881–1942) (Istanbul), who wrote *Esbabi Mucibe Layihasi* [Memorandum on Statement of Reasons] in support of Law Nr. 2510, elaborated on this understanding. In his note dated 2 May 1932, Dr Saydam wrote that, during its earlier phases, the Ottoman Empire had implemented a successful Turkization strategy and that its resettlement policies had been an important part of this assimilationist vision of the Empire. Yet, when the non-Turkish Muslims had been given privileges later on, their assimilation had been curtailed. In addition, during the era of "reverse migration," the "artificial Ottomanization" process of the Tanzimat era had hindered the Turkization of such elements because "a conscious assimilation policy towards the resettlement of these masses" had not been followed. Serious attempts had not been made to integrate the non-Turkish Muslims into the Turkish culture and nation. Now this problem needed to be addressed. Saydam concluded: "It is time to enhance the Turkish population through state-led measures."[51]

The document *Iskan Kanunu Muvakkat Encümen Mazbatasi* [Official Report by the Temporary Committee of the TBMM for the Resettlement Law] also touched on the issue of the assimilation of the Muslim minorities. This report, dated 27 May 1934, cited Albanians, Circassians, and the Abkhazes as examples of Muslim groups that had failed to assimilate into the Turkish nation. Although these immigrants "belonged to the Muslim community and were joined with the Turkish race in their faith," they had not yet become part of Turkish culture. Now the Turkish Republic had to integrate them. Taking "unity in ideals, unity in mind and, first and foremost, unity in language as the basis of the nation," Ankara needed to "amalgamate and alleviate the domestic and transboundary forces of Turkishness." It was the "Turkish Republic's goal and ideal to link everything to the great Turk."[52]

Subsequently, the policy during the 1930s toward non-Turkish Muslim immigrants was to assimilate them. Ankara was aware that, sometimes, non-Turks had been resettled on their own into separate villages and had not assimilated into Turkishness.[53] Those people who "spoke alien dialects" had been able to stand apart from the Turkish nation. Now it was deemed necessary to ascertain those villages in which such "alien dialects" lived and then to distribute populations which spoke the "alien dialects" to Turkish villages nearby (Bayrak 1993: p. 508).

In short, the government's policy vis-à-vis Muslim immigrants who were not Turkish was to resettle them in the midst of the Turks and thereby dilute their ethnic concentration. A subsequent article of the Resettlement Law pointed in this direction by stipulating that those people "whose mother tongue is not Turkish might not establish towns, villages, and worker or artisan units."[54] The preceding analysis of immigration policies in inter-war Turkey shows that the Kemalist state enforced these legal clauses with vigor in order to actualize and promote its understanding of Turkishness.

Hierarchy for immigration to Turkey

The Kemalist immigration policies emphasized the role of race as well as nationality-through-religion in the definition of the Turkish nation. The document *Iskan Muafiyetleri Nizamnamesi* [Statute on Exemptions from Settlement], an executive act from the 1930s that went into effect on 27 December 1934, supported this suggestion (BCA 030.18.1.2/ 50.88.13. 27 December 1934). The statute asserted that those people who "belonged to the Turkish race and culture" and "maintained their Turkish citizenship but lived in other countries" were to be accepted as immigrants to Turkey.[55] Furthermore, Article 3 of the statute, which instructed the Turkish consular offices on issuing visas to aspiring immigrants, stipulated that "people who belong to the Turkish race" might be given immigration visas without approval from the Ministry of Interior, so long as they were not in need of material help upon their arrival in Turkey. However, "those people who share the Turkish culture but do not belong to the Turkish race" might not be issued immigration visas without approval from the Ministry of Interior, even if they declared that they would need no material help upon arrival in Turkey.[56]

What defined the Kemalist concept of race? Another executive act from the 1930s, *Iskan ve Nüfus Islerinin Suratle Ikmali Hakkinda Tamim* [Circular on the Speedy Disposal of Resettlement and Population Matters], helps answer this question. This circular used ethnicity as a lens with which to view the candidates for Turkish citizenship. The circular commanded the local authorities swiftly to provide naturalization certificates to those immigrants who had not yet been naturalized. Its fourth article stipulated that "those people who belong to the Turkish race, or share the Turkish culture, speak Turkish, and know no other languages" should receive their naturalization certificates without inspection.[57] Pomaks, Bosnian Muslims, Crimean Tatars, and Karapapaks should be treated likewise. As for Muslim Georgians, Lezgis, Chechens, Circassians, and Abkhazes, these people could get their papers only after having been investigated by the Ministry of Interior. On the other hand, Kurds, Arabs, Albanians, and other non-

Turkish speaking Muslims, as well as Christians and Jews, were not to receive naturalization certificates or immigrant papers.

This established five hierarchical categories among aspiring Turkish citizens. The first category included ethnic Turks, defined primarily by reference to language, who were entitled to receive naturalization papers immediately. The second group included the Crimean Tatars and Karapapaks, who were welcome by virtue of their ethnic relationship to the Turks. The third category comprised the Balkan Muslims, specifically the Pomaks and the Bosnians. Though not ethnically Turkish, they were viewed as candidates for quick assimilation, as they lacked strong national movements or independent states with which they could identify. Consequently, they were to receive their papers on the spot. The fourth category included the Muslims of the Caucasus: Georgians, Lezgis, Chechens, Circassians, and Abkhazes. Like the Pomaks and the Bosnians, these people also did not have independent homelands. Moreover, with the exception of the Circassians, they, too, were numerically small groups without strong nationalist movements. However, there still were vestiges of nomadism among peoples of this category, and Ankara disfavored nomadism. Combined with its preference for the Balkans over the Caucasus, the Republic exerted caution towards the Muslims of the Caucasus and, as a result, these immigrants could receive their papers only after having been investigated.

In addition, watchfulness over communism also was a factor in Turkey's aversion towards the Muslims of the Caucasus. During the 1930s, Ankara was wary about communism and possible espionage activities by such Muslims from the USSR. Consequently, on 2 November 1937, the government ordered that refugees from the Soviet Union were not to be admitted entry into Turkey. In fait accompli cases, those people who managed to enter the country were to be "resettled at least fifty kilometers away from the Soviet border" (BCA 030.18.1.2/ 79.89.1. 2 November 1937).

The last category in the hierarchy for immigration included the Armenians and other Christians, Jews, Kurds, and various other Muslims, who were not to receive naturalization papers under any circumstances. Of these people, the Christians and the Jews landed on this list of non-desirables for a simple reason: Turkey wanted to see its population diminish, not increase. The Muslims in this group were those people whom the Turkish Republic considered to be difficult to assimilate and, hence, a potential threat. The Albanians and the Arabs had independent states and strong nationalist movements, which meant that their assimilation would not proceed smoothly. Finally, yet importantly, the Republic was especially careful towards the Kurds, the second largest and the least assimilated ethnic group in Turkey. To arrest the growth of its own Kurdish community, Turkey banned the Kurds from immigration.

Conclusion: Three zones of Turkishness under high Kemalism

It appears that Kemalism in the 1920s and the 1930s offered three definitions of the Turkish nation. The first of them was territorial, an idea embodied in the Turkish Constitution of 1924, which registered all inhabitants of Turkey as Turks. This act promised to accommodate the Kurds, the Armenians, and all others as equal citizens of the Republic. The second definition, less inclusive than the first, was religious. As a legacy of the *millet* system, the Kemalists saw all Muslims in Turkey as Turks. This was best demonstrated by the overall tone of the Kemalist immigration regime that facilitated the immigration of Ottoman Muslims in the Balkans. This definition had an internal conflict: although all Turks were Muslims, not all Muslims were Turkish-speaking.

The third, and least inclusive, definition was ethno-religious. First, Kemalists saw only ethnic Turks, determined by their mother tongue, as Turkish. Second, they used religion to classify the non-Turks into two hierarchical categories as Muslims and non-Muslims. They favored the former over the latter. Ethnic Turks were not a solid majority in Turkey. If the Kurds and the other Muslims assimilated, they could enhance the Turkish population. For this reason, helped by the legacy of the *millet* system, the Kemalists were willing to accept the Kurds as Turks if they adopted the Turkish language, albeit without forgetting that they were not in reality ethnically Turkish. Accordingly, Kemalists carefully screened them to prevent their number from increasing and their national identity from blossoming. Paradoxically, such moves may have strengthened the Kurds' national identity.

Kemalism had a less accepting attitude towards non-Muslims. Its praxis treated them as unsuitable for assimilation since they lacked the sine qua non of Turkishness: Islam. Hence, it was religion that created an ethnic boundary between them and the Turks. Turkish nationalism remained hostile to the Christians, whom Turkey marginalized as a community.

It appears that Turkish nationalism during Atatürk's reign produced three concentric zones of Turkishness: an outer territorial one, a middle religious one, and an inner ethnic one. In this scheme, only a group located in the innermost ethnic zone enjoyed close proximity to and the full protection of the Turkish state. Alternatively, the farther away a group was from the center, the more unaccommodating was the Turkish state towards it. Moreover, while groups from the religious layer were expected to move eventually into the inner ethnic core, groups from the territorial zone were strictly confined to the margins of Turkish society.

This state of affairs in Turkey during the 1930s was not unique to the country. Other former Ottoman states, such as Greece, also adhered to ethno-religious nationalisms during the 1930s.[58] As a result of the salience of the *millet* system and ethno-religious identities in the former Ottoman lands, religion became a marker of nationality in the former Ottoman states in the Balkans, as well as Turkey. Hence, today most people in Turkey see all Muslims as Turks, regardless of their ethnicity or language, and all non-Muslims as non-Turks, even when they speak Turkish. This is a crucial conclusion which points at religion's central role in defining nationality in post-Ottoman societies, even in secular Turkey.

Yet what is also interesting is how the recent European Union (EU) accession process has started a remolding of notions of nationality and citizenship in Turkey. In recent years, Ankara has moved fast to satisfy the EU's accession rules, the Copenhagen Criteria, which stipulate, among other things, "respect for minorities."[59] This has started a process in the country that has involved a sincere debate on granting undifferentiated treatment and wider rights to the non-Muslim communities, as well as facilitating education and broadcasting in Kurdish and other languages spoken by various Muslim communities. Even if the deeply entrenched Kemalist notion of Turkishness may prove itself sturdy in the face of any possible erosion, the EU process may yet become the biggest likely recalibration of Turkish nationalism since the 1930s.

Notes

1   For a collection of articles on nationalism and authoritarianism in various European countries in the inter-war era, including Poland, Hungary, Romania, Yugoslavia, and Bulgaria, see Joseph Rothschild (1998). For an excellent work which examines nationalism in inter-war eastern European states including Greece and Bulgaria, see Ivo Banac and Kathryn Verdery (1995).

2   Although the practices of the inter-war Turkish state have been ignored so far, refreshing works recently have appeared on this topic. For examples, see Rifat N. Bali (1999, 2001) and Ayhan Aktar (2000).

3   Between 1876 and 1927 alone, a total of nearly two million Muslim immigrants arrived from the Balkans and the Black Sea basin (Behar 1996: p. 51, p. 62). For more on the persecution of the Ottoman Muslims and their ensuing flight to Anatolia, see Justin McCarthy (1995).

4   In 1935, the Turkish population was roughly 16 million, 98 percent of which were Muslims. Turkish was the first language, spoken by roughly 14 million people (86 percent), and Kurdish the second, spoken by 1.5 million people (9 percent). The other Muslim groups included speakers of Abkhaz (a north-west Caucasus language), Albanian, Arabic, Bosnian (including the Serbian and Croatian variants),

Circassian, Georgian, Persian, Pomak (Bulgarian), and (Crimean) Tatar. See *Istatistik Yilligi* 1938–9: pp. 64–5.

5 For more on the territorial definition of the Turkish nation during the Kemalist era, see Frank Tachau (1972).

6 Turkey's Constitution. Translation into English of the Turkish Constitution of 1924, embodying such amendments to the text as have been made to date, c.1937.

7 *Cumhuriyet Halk Firkasi Nizamnamesi* [By-Laws of the Republican People's Party] (1927, p. 5).

8 Turkey's Constitution. Translation into English of the Turkish Constitution of 1924 (p. 9).

9 Turkish nationalization under Islam's influence resembled the definition of a nation-through-religion by most Balkan nationalist movements. See David Kushner (1977: p. 57). The association of religion with nationality was due to the legacy of the *millet* system. This system had divided the Ottoman population into strict religious compartments, called *millets*. Before the modern era, the system's duration and overarching compartments had merged the pre-modern identities of the Ottoman peoples into religious ones. In the age of nationalisms, these pre-modern identities resurfaced, however, under a religious–ethnic rubric. Subsequently, most Ottoman *millets* were transformed into nations during the last phases of the empire.

10 *Atatürk'ün Söylev ve Demeçleri, I–III* [Ataturk's Speeches and Declarations, I–III] (1997: pp. 74–5).

11 According to the 1927 census, the Kurds constituted a majority of the population in seven provinces of south-eastern Turkey. In these provinces, the largest majority was in Van, where the Kurds formed 79.1 percent of the population. In addition to these provinces, the Kurds made up significant minority communities in another seven Turkish provinces in eastern Turkey (see *Istatistik Yilligi* 1934–5: pp. 160–1).

12 For more on the "Turkish History Thesis," see *Birinci Türk Tarih Kongresi* (1933). The Thesis was inspired by the works of various west European scholars, among them Eugene Pittard (1924). For a contemporary work that deals succinctly with the "Turkish History Thesis," see Büsra Ersanli (2003).

13 The Turkish archives hold an extensive collection of documents on Muslim immigration to Turkey during the 1920s from various parts of the Ottoman Empire and beyond. On immigration from Yemen and Finland, see *Basbakanlik Cumhuriyet Arsivi* [Prime Ministry's Republican Archives]: BCA 272.11/46.79.3. 6 October 1925 and BCA 272.11/53.124.9. 12 May 1927. On Trans-Jordan, see: Great Britain Foreign Office, Political Departments: General Correspondence from 1906. Turkey. FO 371/20091/E1296. Hathorn (Amman) to Thomas (London), 7 March 1936.

14 For the treaty with Armenia, signed on 2 December 1920, see Ismail Soysal (1983: pp. 19–23). For the 31 May 1925 agreement with Albania, consult *TBMM Zabit Ceridesi*, session II, vol. 2, pp. 131–7. For the treaty with Bulgaria, signed on 18 October 1925, see Soysal (1983: pp. 255–9). For the text of the 1923 treaty with Greece, see *Iskan Tarihçesi* 6 (pp. 8–13). For the 1936 treaty with Romania, consult "Türkiye ile Romanya Arasinda Münakid Dobrucadaki Türk Ahalinin Muhaceretini Tanzim Eden Mukavelenamenin Tasdiki Hakkindaki Kanun" [Law to Ratify the Treaty Cosigned by Turkey and Romania to Regulate the Emigration of the Turkish Population in the Dobrudja] Nr. 3102, 25 January 1937, *Düstur*, 3rd. ed., vol. 18, pp. 252–70.

15 FO 371/17963/E7281. Loraine (Angora) to Simon (London), 5 December 1934; FO 371/13092/E3058. Dodd (Sophia) to Chamberlain (London), 18 June 1928.

16 FO 424/268/E129. Clerk (Constantinople) to Chamberlain (London), 4 January 1928.

17 *Iskan Kanunu* [Resettlement law] Nr. 885, 31 May 1926, *Düstur*, 3rd. ed., vol. 7, p. 1441.

18 *TBMM Zabit Ceridesi*, session II, vol. 25, pp. 649–53.

19 The resettlement of the Kurds among the Turks was not a novelty. This had been a popular measure earlier. Especially during its later phases, the Ottoman Empire had resorted to the resettlement of the Kurds in order to assimilate and pacify them, while promoting economic growth and increasing the Muslim ratio in different parts of Anatolia. Fuat Dündar (2001: pp. 137–54) gives a succinct summary of these policies in his work.

20 FO 371/14578/E? Drummond (Geneva) to Cadogan (London), 18 November 1930. *Note sur un entretien avec S. E. Tewfik Rouschdy Bey.*

21 *Iskan Tarihçesi* (p. 137).

22 *Bazi Eshasin Sark Menatikindan Garp Vilayetlerine Nakillerine Dair Kanun* [Law on the Transfer of Certain People from the Eastern Regions to the Western Provinces], Nr. 1097, 17 July 1927, in Naci Kökdemir (1952: pp. 28–30).

23 FO 371/14579/E3898. Clerk (Constantinople) to Henderson (London), 21 July 1930.

24 FO 371/13828/E3538. Clerk (Constantinople) to Henderson (London), 15 July 1929. *Enclosure in no. 1, Notes on a Journey from Angora to Aleppo, Diarbekir, Malatia, Sivas and the Black Sea Coast*, 9–29 June 1929.

25 FO 371/13090/E129. Clerk (Constantinople) to Chamberlain (London), 9 January 1928.

26 Records of the Department of State Relating to the Internal Affairs of Turkey 1930–1944. SD 867.00/2047. Buxley (Izmir) to the State Department (Washington), 3 October 1930, News of Izmir September 1930.

27 FO 371/17958/E4912. Catton (Mersina) to Loraine (Angora), 7 July 1934.

28 *Iskan Kanunu* Nr. 2510, 13 June 1934, *Düstur*, 3rd. ed., vol. 15, addenda, pp. 1156–75. For the text and discussions of this law in the Turkish parliament, see *TBMM Zabit Ceridesi*, session IV, vol. 23, pp. 67–85, 140–66, 189.

29 *TBMM Zabit Ceridesi*, session IV, vol. 23, p. 67.

30 *Iskan Kanunu* Nr. 2510, (p. 1156).

31 *Iskan Kanunu* Nr. 2510, (p. 1156). According to Ismail Besikçi (1977: p. 133), the Zone 3 areas mandated by this article included the following regions: Agri, Sason, Tunceli, Zeylan (Van), southern sections of Kars, parts of Diyarbakir, and sections of Bingöl, Bitlis, and Mus.

32 *Iskan Kanunu* Nr. 2510 (pp. 1159–60).

33 The Inspectorates-General (Umumi Mufettislikler) were regional governorships whose authority prevailed over all civilian, military, and judicial institutions under their domain in large areas of the country. Throughout the 1920s and the 1930s, four of them were established in eastern and south-eastern Turkey, as well as along the eastern Black Sea Coast and in Thrace. For more on the Inspectorates, see Soner Cagaptay (2003a).

34 *Birinci Iskan Mintikalarinda Toprak Tevziatina dair olan Talimatnamenin Kabulü hakkinda Kararname* [Decree Concerning the Adoption of the Executive Act on Land Distribution in the First Resettlement Zones], Nr. 2/12374, 24 November 1939, in Kökdemir (1952: pp. 166–70).

35 *Iskan Kanunu* Nr. 2510 (pp. 1159–60).

36 *Iskan Kanununun 12. Maddesini Kismen Degistiren ve 17. ve 23. Maddelerine Birer Fikra Ekleyen Kanun* [Law Adding Additional Paragraph to Articles 17 and 23 and

Partially Amending Article 12 of the Resettlement Law], Nr. 3667, 5 July 1939, *Düstur*, 3rd. ed., vol. 20, p. 1556.

37 *Birinci Iskan Mintikalarinda Toprak Tevziatina* in Kökdemir (1952: pp. 166–71).

38 In 1934, for instance, while the population density per square kilometer was 68 people in the eastern Black Sea littoral, it was 38 along the Aegean, 35 in the Marmara basin, 32 along the west Black Sea coast, 25 in Thrace, 22 in Central Anatolia, 15 in north-eastern Anatolia, and, finally, 11 within the First Inspectorate-General; see *Iskan Kanunu Muvakkat Encümen Mazbatasi* [Official Report by the Temporary Commission for the Law of Resettlement], *TBMM Zabit Ceridesi*, session IV, vol. 23, addenda 189, p. 6.

39 For the text of this report, see "Report for Reform in the East," quoted in Mehmet Bayrak (1993: pp. 481–9).

40 *Iskan Kanunu* Nr. 2510 (p. 1158).

41 *Iskan Kanunu* Nr. 2510 (p. 1150).

42 *Iskan Kanunu* Nr. 2510 (pp. 1165–6).

43 *Iskan Kanunu* Nr. 2510 (p. 1158).

44 FO 371/16983/E529. Embassy (Constantinople) to the Foreign Office (London), 27 January 1933. *Annual Report for 1932*.

45 *Basvekalet Toprak ve Iskan Isleri Genel Müdürlügü Çalismalari* (Ankara 1955: pp. 108–9), quoted in Ilhan Tekeli (1990, pp. 49–55).

46 *Iskan Kanunu* Nr. 2510 (pp. 1157–8).

47 *TBMM Zabit Ceridesi*, session IV, vol. 23, p. 145.

48 For the changes in its meaning over time, see the word "race" in *The American Heritage Dictionary of the English Language*, Boston: American Heritage Publishing, 1975, p. 1075.

49 *Iskan Kanunu* Nr. 2510 (p. 1157).

50 FO 371/17970/E6434. Morgan (Constantinople) to the Foreign Office (London), 13 October 1934. Minutes by C. W. Baxter, 3 November 1934.

51 *TBMM Zabit Ceridesi*, session IV, vol. 23, addenda 189, pp. 1–2.

52 *TBMM Zabit Ceridesi*, session IV, vol. 23, addenda 189, p. 6.

53 See a confidential decree of September 1930, quoted in Bayrak (1993: pp. 506–9).

54 *Iskan Kanunu* Nr. 2510 (p. 1159).

55 *Iskan Muafiyetleri Nizamnamesi* [Statute on Exemptions from Resettlement], Nr. 2/1777, 27 October 1934, *Düstur*, 3rd. ed., vol. 16, p. 523.

56 *Iskan Muafiyetleri Nizamnamesi* [Statute on Exemptions from Resettlement], Nr. 2/1777, 27 October 1934, *Düstur*, 3rd. ed., vol. 16, p. 521.

57 *Iskan ve Nüfus Islerinin Süratle Ikmali Hakkinda Tamim* [Circular on the Speedy Disposition of Resettlement and Population Matters], Nr. 15035/6599, 7 August 1934, in Kökdemir (1952: pp. 235–6).

58 For instance, a symmetrical situation existed in Greece, where Athens marginalized the non-Orthodox minorities in the country, including the Muslim Turks, Pomaks, Chamuria Albanians, and Roma, as well as the Sephardic Jews and the Catholics. While Greece exercised controls over immigration policy as any other state would, the nature of these controls meant that Athens discriminated against non-Orthodox populations. For more on similarities on the role of religion shaping nationality policies in inter-war Turkey and Greece, see Soner Cagaptay (2003b).

59 "Accession Criteria," representation of the European Commission to Turkey, European Union in Turkey, at http://www.deltur.cec.eu.int/english/enlarge-accession.html. For more on the recent EU reforms in Turkey, see Soner Cagaptay (2003c).

5   The nation in Israel

Between democracy and ethnicity

Alain Dieckhoff

The Declaration of Independence of the State of Israel, read out by David Ben Gurion on May 14 1948, bears traces of the heated discussions which accompanied its composition. The Zionist leaders disagreed as much about the procedure for legitimizing the State as about the political regime to be established. In order to preserve a maximal consensus in the Jewish camp at a time when the first armed confrontation with the Arab States was about to begin, the compilers of the Declaration chose the path of generalized compromise. Thus, the creation of the new State is justified by simultaneous appeals to the voluntarism of the pioneers who had revived Hebrew and established the kibbutzim, the distress resulting from the Shoah, international law (the Balfour declaration of 1917, the UNO partition plan of 1947), the principle of self-determination, and historical rights based on the inseparable tie between the Jewish people and the Land of Israel.

This same concern for wide appeal appears again in the invocation, at the end of the text, of the protection of the "Rock of Israel": a metaphorical expression that is sufficiently imprecise to allow religious people to understand "God" when agnostics understand "the Jewish people." This wish to reach an amicable agreement is evident in the very name of the new State. The title "Kingdom of Israel," by which ancient Israel was known up to the coronation of Saul, would have implied the establishment of a community ruled by divine law: an objective immediately rejected by the immense majority of Zionists. On the other hand, to speak of the "Republic of Israel" was unacceptable to the religious parties, since they believed that monarchy was sure to be restored with the advent of messianic times. So the compromise formula "State of Israel" (*Medinat Israel*) was preferred, some seeing this as a modern governmental structure, and others as an essential element in the spiritual mission of the Jewish people. From its very act of foundation, the State of Israel presents, like Janus, two faces: as a product of political secularization, it belongs resolutely to the present day; as the sign of a religious testimony, it belongs to an immemorial past. This hybrid character of the State involves much more than the mere political will to obtain the widest possible consensus: it reflects the inherent ambivalence of the Zionist national program.

In its beginnings, at the end of the nineteenth century, the Zionist solution as conceived by Theodor Herzl had a single aim: to give Jews political sovereignty by creating an independent State. The State was conceived as an instrument of protection, which would free the Jews from the constraints of anti-Semitism by providing them a "political home" of their own. The intention, which was restated over and over again by Herzl, was not to create a Jewish State, where the collective life would be impregnated by Judaism, but a State for the Jews, where they would be in the majority and therefore politically dominant, without, however, contesting the equality of all citizens. The Herzlian model is a liberal democracy in which religion is a private matter that does not affect the public domain.[1]

It is clear, however, that the State of Israel does not correspond to the vision of the man who is nevertheless honoured as its mythic founder. This discrepancy is connected with the reorientation which Herzl's successors, Russian Jews with a strong sense of their special identity, gave to the original program. To them, the independent State ought to be not only a framework for the expression of political sovereignty, but also an instrument to protect a specific culture. In other words, Zionism certainly implied an aspiration for political liberty, but equally, if not more so, for the preservation of a collective identity which even claimed a certain historical continuity.

Zionism is founded on an intrinsic duality. As a democratic movement, it saw the people, and no longer God, as the main agent of Jewish history, invested with political rights rather than religious obligations. This change very naturally aroused vehement opposition from the rabbis, who saw with remarkable acuity that Zionism really involved giving the Jewish people political normality by providing them with a territorialized State structure, and that this would be the end of their exceptional position as a diaspora. On the other hand, as an identity movement, Zionism was based on the reappropriation of structural elements of Jewish identity: such as the triad, Land of Israel, Bible, and Hebrew language. No doubt these references were invested with a patriotic significance, but their very strong religious connotation remained undeniable: a Jewish national identity seemed simply unthinkable without reference, however minimal, to a tradition that was first and foremost a religious one. The impossibility of separating

Zionism from Judaism prevented any clear-cut delinking of the political and religious spheres, since the former could not dispense with the latter in defining the very Jewish identity which they wished to perpetuate. While revolutionary on the political level, Zionism remained thoroughly conservative on the national level.

The Jewishness of the State of Israel

The State of Israel was explicitly created as "a Jewish State in the Land of Israel." This formulation is far from innocuous. It attests that the State which manifests the Jewish people's right of self-determination must have a Jewish character.[2] This fact is underlined by the national symbolism. The blue and white flag, inspired by the traditional prayer shawl, shows the Star of David, while the State emblem is the seven-branched candlestick. These signs, borrowed directly from religious symbolism, do not have the neutrality of the French tricolor flag and the motto of the Republic (liberty, equality, fraternity), which have a universal application. That they have a particularistic meaning could hardly be questioned, were it not for the fact that one Israeli in five experiences real difficulties in identifying with a State that represents itself by these symbols: for the simple reason that he/she is an Arab.

If this Jewishness were simply formal, "anecdotal," few problems would arise; but the fact is that it has significant repercussions on the level of political organization and the very concept of nationality. Thus, the Knesset, the parliamentary assembly elected by universal suffrage, is directly responsible for enacting legislation with a religious coloration. Laws adopted since 1948 regulate, for example, observance for the Sabbath, provision of kosher food to the army, abortion, and forbid, among other things, flights by the national airline *El Al* on Sabbath and festival days, the sale of bread during the Passover, raising pigs and selling pork, and "indecent" advertisements. The public domain is thus partly governed by religious rules which have become legal constraints only by being incorporated into the law of the State.

The social presence of Judaism is reinforced by its institutionalization. Although Judaism is not an official State religion, it undeniably has a special status which assures it a privileged position in the public sphere,[3] much more so than happens in some countries which do have an official religion (the Church of England, for example). A chief Rabbinate with two "primates" (Ashkenazi and Sephardic) heads a "public service of religion" administered by religious officials in State pay and local groups of rabbis who are responsible for ritual bathing, animal slaughter, and the enforcement of food regulations in public eating places. This religious organization is backed up by a judicial apparatus, comprising twelve rabbinical courts and a Court of Appeal, which has sole competence in matters regarding marriage and divorce. In fact, the legislature has ceded the management of Jewish matrimonial matters to the rabbinical courts. This measure was passed in 1953 for pragmatic reasons, when Ben Gurion needed parliamentary backing from the religious parties, which have always played a crucial supporting role in coalitions in Israel. But the real reason for it is a much deeper one: although Zionism aspired to give a new political basis to the lives of modern Jewry, it found it impossible to define the national tie that unites Jews on any other grounds than religious criteria. By handing over to the rabbis the management of personal status, Israel's secular leaders have implicitly acknowledged, although with great reluctance, the correctness of the religious objection that had always affirmed the indissolubility of the link between nation and religion in Judaism.

This rabbinical monopoly, which makes any marriage between Jew and non-Jew legally impossible in Israel, is evidently incompatible with the respect for individual liberties which ought to be upheld by any democratic State. Its only justification is that it keeps intact an ancient religious bond which takes the place of a national bond. By reserving for themselves exclusive control over family law, the Orthodox rabbis have not received a simple unimportant concession. On the contrary: they have gained control over the core of society. The Orthodox monopoly over marriage has not been significantly undermined. Indeed, the two other branches of Judaism (Reform and Conservative) cannot have the marriages celebrated by their rabbis in Israel that are recognized by the Ministry of the Interior and the Rabbinate. They have to resort to indirect ways like the organization of offshore "Love Boat" weddings, outside the territorial waters of Israel in a civil ceremony carried out by the ship's captain and followed by a shipboard Conservative or Reform wedding ceremony. As for marriages which cannot be legally celebrated in Israel (i.e. between a Jew and a non-Jew), the engaged couple has to marry abroad or in some foreign consulate in Israel; according to international private law a State (here, Israel) has to recognize marriages performed according to the civil law of foreign states.

The legislation over marriage stresses the salience of Jewishness as a structural foundation of Israel, a fact which is further epitomized by the Law of Return (1950) which gives to every Jew, anywhere in the world, the right to immigrate to Israel (freedom of immigration is only restricted for people who had an activity directed against the Jewish people, or are likely to endanger public health or the security of the State, or have a criminal past which endangers public welfare). Freedom of immigration constitutes the most obvious expression of the State of Israel's mission of "ingathering the exiles." However, once this general principle has been acknowledged, it remains to determine who may take advantage of it. In other words, who is a Jew?

In a State which officially claims to be Jewish, the actual definition of Jewishness has caused many problems. This question has given rise to numerous disputes relating to the civil registration of the religious status (*dat*) and ethno-national origin (*leom*) of Israeli residents. Up to 1970, the State frequently allowed children whose father alone was Jewish to be registered as Jews under the heading "leom." This practice, which led to abundant legal disputes, was unacceptable to the traditionalists because it contravened the religious law which acknowledges as Jews only individuals whose mother is Jewish or have been duly converted. In 1970, they finally succeeded in getting the definition of Jewish nationality to correspond strictly to the religious definition. The nation–religion equation was thus once more strengthened, although it is still not total. Indeed, the text of the 1970 law in fact also recognized as Jewish "one who has converted to Judaism," without, however, elaborating the procedure to be followed. The question was then to determine whether a new immigrant, converted to Judaism in the diaspora by Reform or Conservative rabbis, who are less strict than their Orthodox colleagues, would be allowed to benefit from the right to return and be registered as a Jew by the Ministry of the Interior. To the great displeasure of the orthodox, the Supreme Court replied in the affirmative. This dissonance, which hardly comes up in practice, does not however diminish the monopoly of the Orthodox rabbinate over the definition of Jewishness.

This matter of assigning Jewish identity is of the greatest importance because it provides entitlement to significant rights. Every Jew who settles in Israel is allowed generous tax relief during the first years, loans at reduced interest, and various other kinds of help to facilitate integration. But above all, he/she automatically receives Israeli citizenship by the simple fact of having decided to return to "his own country."[4] This major concession, closely connected with the right of return, constitutes the most striking manifestation of the Jewishness of the State of Israel, which is also clearly revealed by the status of its national institutions.

Before the establishment of the State, three organizations played an essential part in promoting the Zionist cause: the World Zionist Organisation/Jewish Agency, responsible for politically promoting the establishment of a Jewish State and providing concrete aid to immigrants settling in Palestine; the Keren Hayessod, which collected funds amongst the Jewish diaspora; and the Jewish National Fund, responsible for the purchase of land. Should, after 1948, all these tasks be transferred to the sovereign State of Israel? The last preferred to maintain these "national institutions" in existence, while at the same time giving legal form to its relationships with them (in three laws of 1952, 1953, and 1956). This decision was taken in order to preserve institutional links with the Jews of the diaspora, but above all because these institutions, which existed to work for the Jewish people, served the interests of Israeli Jews alone: and not of the Arab citizens of Israel.

The Jewish Agency, for example, not only supplies new immigrants with many forms of assistance; it also creates whole villages for Jews, finances water and electricity connections, and fosters the development of agriculture and industry. Though it may be found acceptable that the Jewish Agency, whose funds come from voluntary donations of Jews in the diaspora, is active in improving conditions for Jews alone, it is nevertheless obvious that this one-sided assistance increases disparities with and resentments among the 1.2 million Arab citizens of the State.

The problematic nature of the "national institutions" can best be seen in connection with the Jewish National Fund (JNF) and its role in de-Arabizing the land. In 1948, after almost half a century in existence, the JNF had purchased 4.5 percent of the land in Palestine. After Israel's military victory in the first Israeli–Arab war, its possessions rose suddenly to 18 percent of the land in Israel. Most of the "abandoned land," which belonged to the 750,000 Arabs who had fled Palestine during the fighting, was in fact transferred to the JNF, which applied to them the principle of non-availability which governs its activities: not only could these lands, as the "perpetual property of the Jewish people," not be re-sold to any private party, but they could not even be let out to a non-Jew. By interposing these national institutions (voluntary organizations financed by the diaspora), the State had discovered an ideal way of giving preferential treatment to Jews, without itself officially violating the principle of the equality of all citizens.[5]

The Jewishness of the State, which leads directly or indirectly to preferential treatment for Jews, is an almost constitutional axiom which the Knesset confirmed in 1985 by decreeing that any party that contested the existence of the State of Israel as the State of the Jewish people could not participate in elections. If a party presented itself to the electors with a demand for abrogation of the Law of Return, for example, it would be disqualified. This Jewishness of the State, which is constantly reaffirmed, is not just imposed from above; it enjoys wide consensus among the Jewish population of Israel. The "Canaanite" movement, which from 1940 to 1950 advocated a secular State of Israel without any institutional links to Judaism and the Jewish diaspora, was very much a minority affair (Diamond 1986). Even if the secularization of the State has a wider appeal today, particularly among the liberal left, most Israelis remain firmly committed to the Zionist mission of the State, as was shown in 1989–90 by the nationwide enthusiasm about the wave of Jewish immigration from the Soviet Union.

Zionism: Building a nation

The outstanding importance of migration in Israeli history highlights the constructed character of the Jewish nation in Israel. Contrary to the vehement proclamations of nationalist ideologues, no nation has an eternal existence, the Jewish nation no more than the French or German nations. To take shape, a nation must become, through the mediation of its intelligentsia, precisely that imaginary community whose members feel that they belong to the same whole. This work of national construction, which is always delicate, was complicated further in the Zionist case by a double handicap. On one hand, the ancestral homeland had been inhabited for hundreds of years by a population with an Arabic culture, which was demographically much more numerous (in 1880 Arabs numbered about 450,000, Jews 25,000) and owned 99 percent of all private land. On the other hand, Jews were a dispersed people, who lacked a common language and were living in extremely diverse socio-political environments. In these conditions, Zionism embarked on a truly titanic task: to establish political sovereignty over a land which Jews no longer legally owned, at the same time convincing all of them to gather in Zion. The Zionist program thus required a widespread transfer of landed property (an important point that we shall return to) and systematic immigration, without which the Jewish territorialized nation could never have been constituted.

Today there are 5.1 million Jews in Israel, several times as many as when the State was founded. This demographic increase is very largely due to the immigration of three million people, mainly from Islamic countries and eastern Europe (including the former USSR). The "ingathering of the exiles," the creed of Zionism, was an indispensable precondition for the creation of a Jewish nation, but was in itself obviously insufficient. The ideological postulate of the perennial unity of the Jewish people in fact came up against a sociological reality that was much more diversified. The Jewish people, whose cohesion was proclaimed by Zionist leaders, had become extremely varied, both socially and culturally, in the course of its two thousand years of dispersion. Certainly the Jews had maintained their membership of a particular religion, and this kept up a sort of common feeling among them, but although this might be the basis for a sort of natural ("tribal") unity, it was not enough to awaken a real national consciousness. Put side by side, for example, an immigrant of German origin, communist, urbanite, and lover of Goethe, and one from the Yemen, illiterate and pastoral: apart from the statement that both of them were born Jews, they have nothing in common. So it was necessary to awaken in them the feeling that their meeting was not just fortuitous or that it was not just connected with troubled historical circumstances, because the first has fled from Nazism, the second from Arab nationalism. Their individual trajectories must take a meaning within a collective project. So the State had to play a decisive role in awakening the will to live together, through two institutions: the school and the army.

The school remains a powerful instrument for the emergence of a common culture, because the medium of instruction is Hebrew (in the Jewish sector). The spread of a common tongue, which has made it possible to overcome the original linguistic "babelization," has given the Jews a strong national cohesion. But the school not only contributes to linguistic and symbolic unification, it also has an essential civic function. The law on national education of 1953 makes clear that instruction should be "based on the values of Jewish culture and scientific achievements, on patriotism and loyalty to the State and the Jewish people." Thus, education is explicitly intended to serve the patriotic ideal. History, literature, and Bible study are used to emphasize the closeness of the connection between the Jewish people and the land of Israel.

In this process of nationalizing the masses, the army plays a role which complements that of the schools, and is in certain respects even more decisive. Let us first recall that conscription is universal (Jewish men and women are called today to serve under the flag for three years and 21 months, respectively) and that soldiers are recalled for periods of obligatory reserve-service up to 54 years of age. The choice of becoming a nation under arms has been preferred because, by making defense of the homeland the common concern of everyone, it has developed the sense of sharing a common destiny within a single national collectivity. This integrating effect of the army is particularly clear in the case of new immigrants, who receive not only military but also general training (courses in Hebrew, and less often, literacy). By playing an active role in the absorption of immigrants and fostering an intense social mixing process, the army has really been the outstanding creator of Israeli identity. Thus, "genuine" Israeliness is subjectively linked, not with citizenship, but with enrolment in the army. Those who do not participate in this military experience (Israeli Arabs who are exempted, ultra-orthodox Jews who get draft deferments) are seen as outside the boundaries of the imagined national community.[6] The Druzes (an heterodox sect originating within Islam which numbers 110,000 people in Israel) are in an intermediary position: they are partially included as the men are subjected to compulsory service, but still on the margins as they are not part of the core group.

The army's centrality in the process of nation-building was further reinforced by the permanent military pressure to which Israel has been subjected by the Arab states. From this point of view, it could be said that, by refusing to recognize the Jewish State for almost half a century, and by choosing on several occasions the path of military confrontation, the neighbouring states have enabled Israel to consolidate its internal cohesion. The feeling of being exposed to an unremitting hostility strengthened Israelis in the sense that, despite their diverse backgrounds, they shared the same destiny. In the organization of the national memory, recollection of these wars has an essential function. Soldiers who have fallen in the defense of the country are honored in military cemeteries, by monuments to the dead, in "remembrance books," and even by a special day of commemoration. This has been set on the day before Independence Day, to emphasize that without the sacrifice of these soldiers the political rebirth of Israel would never have been possible. This commemoration of heroism is also equally present on the day of Remembrance of the Shoah, which certainly honors all victims of the genocide, but also gives a special place to the Zionist fighters in the ghettos. In this way the State of Israel is presented as the perpetuation of this spirit of resistance and the most effective protection against any new Holocaust. (For additional information, see Tom Segev, 1993.)

Thanks to the schools and the army, and also to the constitution of a national memory, the State has succeeded in forging a more "compact" Jewish nation. But, of course, dividing lines remain. For example, in the 1950s, socio-economic disparities corresponded very closely to a communal distinction between Ashkenazis (European and American origin), who constituted the political and economic elite of the country, enjoying a higher standard of living and imposing their European culture, and Sephardim (Jews from the Islamic countries) who were less educated, less well-off, and relegated to the bottom of the social ladder. This communal divergence remains, even if State welfare measures have lessened it. The second big division, between Jews who are Orthodox (about one third of the Jewish population) and those who are less, or not at all, is definitely more persistent. Nevertheless, although conflicts do arise from time to time, for example about the rulings of the Supreme Court, the modus vivendi established in 1947 is maintained in spite of everything.[7] Even if coexistence is far from always being peaceful, given the basic disagreement between religious and secular Jews about the ultimate character of the State (respectively, theocracy versus liberal democracy), the State of Israel is in some way necessarily their State, because it belongs collectively to the Jewish people. The real dividing line thus lies elsewhere: between Jews and non-Jews.

The Arabs in Israel: A national minority

The presence of a significant Arab minority (one-fifth of the total population) is a relic of recent Middle Eastern history. The creation of the State of Israel upon 80 percent of British Palestine territory in 1948–9 led to the exodus of about 750,000 Arabs (Morris 1987). Only 160,000 remained and became Israelis by residence. This demographic upheaval in Palestinian society abruptly transformed the political situation of the Arabs who stayed put: from being members of the majority group, they suddenly became a minority in a Jewish State, which they had opposed with arms. This strange situation placed them in a problematic relationship to both the Palestinian refugees in neighboring Arab countries and to the State of Israel. The former went on reproaching them as cowards and traitors for submitting to Jewish domination rather than leaving "the Zionist entity." The latter established complicated ties with them that were marked by the ambiguity of the State of Israel: a Jewish State, but also a democratic State based formally on the equality in law for all citizens. This last principle figures explicitly in the Declaration of Independence, where the new State promises to ensure "the most complete social and political equality to all inhabitants without distinction of religion, race or sex." Arabs received the right to vote and to stand for election in 1949. But this apparent respect for universal citizenship was immediately counterbalanced by the fact that civil liberties of Arabs were severely restricted.[8]

Up to 1966, they were subject to a military administration which strictly limited their freedom of movement. For example, in 1952, a court fined some parents on behalf of their minor children who, wanting to see the sea, had left their village without permission from the military authorities. House arrests, official detentions (with minimal judicial control), and censure of the Arab press were frequent occurrences during this period. Freedom of political association was subject to innumerable constraints. The al-Ard party, of Nasserist tendency, was not allowed to participate in elections in 1965, on the grounds that its support for Arab nationalism implied denial of the right of the Jewish people to have their own State. Possibilities for the political self-expression of Arabs were even more restricted by the fact that, with the exception of a small leftist group (Mapam), all the Zionist parties, including Ben Gurion's Labour Party, simply did not include Arab members. It is not surprising that under these conditions many Arabs joined the Communist Party, the only openly binational group, which advocated transforming the State of Israel into a community of citizens.

Although some of the measures applied to the Arab population were due to security needs such as the prevention of espionage, control of terrorism, etc., the widespread application of them over a long period and in a collective manner made them into elements of a real system of subordination, which became most forcefully apparent in the granting of citizenship, and in legislation about land rights.[9] Whereas the law on nationality of 1952 accords Israeli citizenship automatically to any Jewish immigrant, it was granted to Arabs only if they had resided without interruption on the territory which became Israel, between 14 May 1948 and the date when the law came into force (i.e. four years). So neither the hundreds of thousands of Palestinian refugees who had left their native villages during the war, nor even several thousand Arabs who had fled temporarily to neighboring countries before returning to what had become Israel, could benefit from this provision. The position of these residents without citizenship was finally settled only as late as 1980 when they finally got Israeli citizenship. Nevertheless, even for the Arabs who did obtain it in their 50s, Israeli citizenship was no protection against the string of land laws which were passed during the 1950s.

The most notorious law is the "Acquisition of Absentees' Property" (1950) which allowed a massive transfer of ownership: not only were all lands and fixed assets of Palestinian refugees and all Islamic Waqf properties transferred to the State via the Custodian for Absentees' Property, the same was done for half of the lands belonging to Israeli Arabs, who, by a truly Orwellian legal fiction, were considered "present absentees" (i.e. although they were present on Israeli territory, they were legally considered absent because they temporarily left their place of residence during the Independence War, 1947–9). As many as 75,000 Arabs became "present absentees."[10] The 1950 law and other legal arrangements (on security and emergency, land acquisition) were of paramount importance in "judaizing" the land. Indeed, in 1948, the State of Israel was in an unusual position: it exercised sovereignty on a country where Jews owned barely 10 percent of the land. As successor State, Israel took over all public lands and lands considered ownerless, but one-third of all the land remained legally the private property of Arabs. The special land expropriation laws had the objective of reducing Arab ownership, in which they were successful: today Arab-owned property covers only 3.5 percent of the total land area, while the State now firmly controls 93 percent (the rest belongs to Jewish private parties). In the matter of land, it is clear that Israeli Arabs have been treated scarcely any better than their fellows who took refuge in Lebanon or Syria. The State considered them first and foremost not as Israeli citizens whose rights must be respected, but as Palestinian Arabs, members of an ethno-national group who had to be turned into a subordinate minority.

No doubt, the objective situation of Israeli Arabs has improved since the 1970s, in all three categories identified by the British sociologist T. H. Marshall: civil rights (freedom of thought, conscience, religion, movement, and so on), political rights (political organization and participation), and social rights. However, those improvements that are due to a more effective Arab political mobilization and to a liberalizing trend of the State system (mainly through the judicial activism of the Supreme Court) cannot conceal the fact that the structural discrimination against the Arab citizens remains a reality and persists on all three levels.

As far as civil rights are concerned, although they are globally respected, when it comes to the restoration of public order, the police have a clear tendency to act very harshly. The tragic events of October 2000, when 13 Israeli Arabs were shot dead by the police during demonstrations launched in solidarity with the Palestinian Intifada in the West Bank and the Gaza Strip, were, in a way, exceptional (it is necessary to go back to 1976 to find such a degree of lethal violence). However, they are also the direct outcome of a general perception which sees the Arabs in Israel as a dangerous fifth column against which repressive measures are legitimate.

Concerning political rights, although the Arabs became much better integrated into the political system, the pressure on political leaders has increased. Thus, the Member of Parliament, Azmi Bishara, head of the National Democratic Alliance, has been deprived of his parliamentary immunity (November 2001) and indicted twice: first, for having traveled to Syria ("an enemy state") and, second, for two public speeches in which he affirmed the right of occupied peoples to resist occupation. He was also disqualified from taking part in the 2003 elections by the Central Elections Committee, but the Israeli Supreme Court overruled the banning. When it comes to the exercise of political power, Arabs remain marginalized. It was only in March 2001 that an Arab became, for the first time, a minister in the Israeli government. Although marking a step in the political inclusion of Arabs, it should not be overestimated: indeed, Salah Tarif, member of the Druze minority, got a ministry without portfolio, devoid of real substance.

Finally, social rights (health, education, welfare) are still not evenly distributed. Jewish schools get more public funding than Arab schools, and public housing construction programs are more numerous in Jewish areas than in Arab ones. Even quotas of water for irrigation are higher for kibbutzim than for neighboring Arab villages. Similarly, the disadvantaged zones for which the State provides specific grants to encourage economic development have been designed in such a way that they do not include a single Arab village.

The Arabs of Israel remain in a situation that is curious, to say the least: on one hand, they are citizens of a State which has given them the right to vote, and has undeniably contributed to a certain socio-economic modernization; on the other, they remain outside the Jewish State, which treats them as aliens.

Israel: An ethnic democracy

The national project to which Zionism gave birth is founded on an ethno-cultural conception of the nation, rather than on a political one. The former view of the nation is not well received in the Western world because it is considered unavoidably inegalitarian. But this is not always the case. Consociational democracies such as Belgium and Switzerland are based on the recognition of communal divisions, which are regulated by the institutionalization of compromise through various procedures: power-sharing between the elites of the major groups, proportional representation for each community within the higher political and administrative levels, veto power for minority groups, direct management by the communities of certain domains (such as education) (Lijphart 1977).

At a first and quick glance, Israel looks like a consociational democracy. Arabs enjoy an institutional autonomy, such as in the existence of an Arab educational system and in the administration of personal status (marriage, divorce) by the religious authorities of the various communities (Muslim, Druze, various Christian denominations). These collective rights are supported and protected by the State. Nevertheless, in Israel, this institutional pluralism does not function in the required setting of a consociational democracy where the State is a neutral authority which treats all communities on an equal footing, each of them having the same right of access to the decision-making bodies. This is manifestly not the case, since the Jewish group is directly linked with the State and is objectively favored. On the other side, this Jewish supremacy does not involve a total monopolization of power, such as the Whites had in South Africa from 1948 to 1994. By allowing Arabs to participate in the democratic process, Israel has explicitly repudiated this type of democracy of "the master-race."

So how can we describe Israel which has at the same time accepted the principle of citizenship on an individual basis, recognized the plurinational nature of its population and set up preferential links between one ethnic group (the Jews) and the State? The answer seems to be: as an "ethnic democracy" where political sovereignty belongs to the Israeli citizens as a whole (and only to them), but where the State is that of the Jewish people (Smooha 1990: pp. 389–413). Such a patchwork is bound to be precarious, since the preponderance of the main group frequently clashes with the equality of all citizens. Up to now, a judicious mixture of control and liberalism has enabled the Israeli ethnic democracy to survive, but how long can this balance be maintained?

On the Jewish side, public opinion, even the most liberal, remains very strongly in favor of the Jewishness of the State. A recent survey shows that Jews overwhelmingly (62.2 percent) prefer that Israel continue to be a Jewish-Zionist State (Smooha 1997: pp. 198–241). Although they think that the lot of the Arab citizens should be improved (better protection of their democratic rights, proportional share of the budget, and so on), they still clearly reject the consociational model that would recognize Jews and Arabs as equal national groups. On the Arab side, mobilization for full equality of rights and an end to discrimination will remain strong. However, the prospects for such an evolution are looking grim. The October 2000 events have increased the mutual alienation between the Arab community and the Jewish majority, a fact which does not predispose the latter to more openness towards Arab claims.

Even the emergence of an independent Palestinian State (a rather distant prospect) will not necessarily be good news for the Arab minority in Israel. Of course, such an outcome will be positively valued from a political point of view (recognition of Palestinian national rights), but it is rather doubtful that it will have an overall positive effect on the specific situation of the Arab citizens of Israel. Why? Because most Israeli Jews will see the creation of a Palestinian State alongside their State as their final contribution to a global settlement while the Arab States and the Arab public will be asked to accept without reservation the existence of Israel as a Jewish-Zionist State. The territorial compromise will thus strengthen the Jewish nature of the State, deepen the estrangement of the Arab citizens of Israel towards it and jeopardize any "de-ethnicization" of Israel. Clearly, the contrasting perspectives of Jews and Arabs on Israel's future will maintain tensions between the two groups and lead to an unstable equilibrium. The advent of an Israeli nation, made up of Jews and Arabs as equal partners in governing the State, is still a very remote dream.

Notes

1 On the different ideological constructions of the Jewish nation in Zionism, see Alain Dieckhoff (2003).
2 For a detailed juridical analysis, see Claude Klein (1977).
3 For an historical and sociological analysis of the position of Judaism in Israel, see Zalman Abramov (1976).
4 The automatic granting of citizenship is also given to the direct relatives of a Jew (spouse, children, grandchildren, and their spouses). This provision was introduced in order to keep "mixed families" united and allow them to immigrate. Nevertheless, this liberal arrangement stresses the ethnic dimension, as the criterion in the kinship with a Jew (up to the second generation), more than the religious affiliation. At work here is an extended ethnicity principle.
5 This massive transfer of lands was first documented by a Palestinian holding Israeli citizenship. See Sabri Jiryis (1968). Later works have confirmed these early findings. See, for instance, David Kretzmer (1990: pp. 49–76).
6 Sara Helman (1997: pp. 305–32). Several people interviewed state that "the army is an integral part of our culture ... an Israeli experience."
7 On these two cleavages, see Alain Dieckhoff (1999: pp. 217–31).
8 For more information about the lot of the Arabs in Israel, see Alain Dieckhoff (1993: pp. 99–106).
9 This control system has been dissected in detail by Ian Lustick (1980).
10 *Nokhehim nifkadim* (present absentees) is the original Hebrew title of the testimonies of Israeli Arabs gathered by the novelist David Grossman (translated into English 1993).

6   A nation divided

Lebanese confessionalism

*Maurus Reinkowski and
Sofia Saadeh**

Since it gained independence in 1943 from the French mandate, Lebanon's political system has had a dual structure. On the one hand, the Lebanese Constitution was modeled after the French, proclaiming equality of all citizens before the law; and on the other hand, alongside this official constitution, a verbal agreement known as the National Pact of 1943 was contracted between the heads of the two major sects at the time, the Muslim Sunnis and the Christian Maronites (al-Khazen 1991). It stipulated a balanced representation of the sects on all echelons of government offices. Thus, in the Lebanese political system rights and entitlements have been allocated according to an individual's confessional affiliation; and personal status laws, as well as the institutions through which these laws are applied, have been under the exclusive control of the religious authorities of Lebanon's officially recognized confessional groups (Khairallah 1994: p. 260). The political life of Lebanese citizens is controlled through the division of power among the most prominent sects, and their private lives through the religious personal status laws of the 18 sects now in existence in Lebanon.[1] In the aftermath of the civil war that raged in Lebanon between 1975 and 1990, a new constitution was written whereby sectarian representation in politics became mandatory, and consequently religious leaders began to share power with the politicians through the control of the personal status of citizens, as well as through the control of the several sectarian militias that had sprung up during the war.

The Lebanese political system would best be defined as "confessionalism," which, in turn, is a subspecies of the more general concept of "consociationalism," a term that refers to states and societies marked by "segmental cleavages [that] may be of a religious, ideological, linguistic, regional, cultural, racial, or ethnic nature."[2] The term "confessionalism" depicts the mechanisms of conflict management and power balance in the political culture of Lebanon, hinting at its deep-rooted traditions of clientelism and clan politics. In the Lebanese confessional system it is not the parties, but the confessional groups (or, to be more precise, the elites of the confessional groups), that have been acknowledged as the main political actors. These political actors resort to mechanisms of conflict resolution and interest balancing by following the criteria of a confessionally defined proportional power-sharing formula. The Lebanese system is probably unique in the way in which political representation necessarily operates through the "confessional" hierarchy in spite the existence of all the institutions of a democratic parliamentary regime.[3] In the following, the term "confessionalism" will be used in order to refer not only to the political procedures which are based on a confessional model of political power-sharing, but also to the whole of the political culture.

The rise of Lebanese confessionalism

Proponents have argued that the Lebanese confessionalist system represents a genuine legacy of Ottoman rule, and that it even dates back to the Mamluk era. Being so deeply rooted in Lebanese political culture, the abrogation of confessionalism would be detrimental to Lebanese state and society.[4] Such an argument is hardly acceptable as it suggests that confessionalism is inscribed into the "national genetic code" of the Lebanese.[5] Furthermore, the record of the post-Ottoman era shows that the confessionalist principle was not necessarily adopted in all of the empire's successor states. Therefore, one should seriously consider Ghassan Salamé's argument (1994: p. 97) that the national pact in the Lebanese republic owed itself to a "quid pro quo of state survival, a protective stratagem on the part of the ruling segment to ensure the state survival." In other words, the confessional regime in Lebanon may be due in part to the calculation of the powerful but not completely dominating Maronites that, without the participation of other confessional groups, they would not be able to retain power in the newly founded Lebanese republic.

Confessionalist institutions and devices were widely practiced all over the Ottoman empire. Why they persisted (or are said to persist) in some successor states, but not in others, must be answered in the context of the formation period of the post-Ottoman states. The early decades of the Lebanese republic were decisive for the internalization and "eternalization" of confessionalism. Besides the Constitution of 1926, in which the principle of confessionalism was anchored in its Article 95, an unwritten gentlemen's agreement was arranged in 1943 by the leaders of the Maronite and Sunni communities (Bishara Khuru and Riyad Sulh). The now abrogated Article 95 (as modified by the Constitutional Law of 1943) read as follows: "As a transitory measure and for the sake of even justice and concord, the communities shall be equally represented in public posts and in ministerial composition, without damage to State interest resulting therefrom."[6] The "national pact" of 1943 consisted of a number of mutual guarantees. Whereas the Christians renounced their quest for protection from the Western powers, the Muslims withdrew from the idea of a possible absorption into Syria or a still to be realized Arab union. Lebanon was defined as a "country with an Arab face and Arab language," yet with a "special character."

It was further agreed to divide the power, that is the major political positions and administrative responsibilities, on a proportional basis among the six largest communities: Maronite, Greek Orthodox, Greek Catholic, Sunni, Shi'i, and Druze. Based on data from the last national census of 1932, seats in parliament were distributed on the multiple of 11: for each six Christian deputies, the chamber would include five Muslim and Druze. In government and civil service, the ratio would be 50:50. The Maronites held the presidency and the command of the army, the office of prime minister went to the Sunnis, the presidency of the parliament to the Shi'is, and the vice-presidency to the Greek Orthodox. Certain posts were reserved for other confessional groups, such as the Ministry of Defense for the Druze. The national pact thus represented a compromise among elites seeking to secure the benefits from their positions of power. The Lebanese people "were clearly not consulted and the system that was adopted had the effect of keeping them in the communal framework under the thumb of the traditional notables, heads of families, landowners, and clerical authorities."[7]

Nevertheless, state authorities and even political scientists predicted in the decades following 1943 that confessionalism in Lebanon would be a transitory phenomenon. As in other consociationalist states such as the Netherlands and Austria, a full-fledged democratic culture would sooner or later blossom. Instead, Lebanon came into the grip of a protracted and woeful civil war (1975–90) caused by a complicated amalgam of external and internal factors. In the 1980s and 1990s, the search for the origins of the civil war triggered a debate on the part that confessionalism had played in it. Two opposing schools of interpretation clearly stand out. According to the first, certainly the minoritarian one, the Lebanese political system would have been able to sustain and handle the internal class and political conflicts if there had not been the intrusion of external conflicts and pressures into Lebanon (e.g. Hanf 1993). The other, and more widely accepted, interpretation is that the fragile and increasingly more paralyzing process of consensus-seeking, combined with stark socio-economic inequalities, not only made Lebanon vulnerable to external influences but also was so unstable that any potential disturbance (which already is in abundance in that region) would have driven Lebanon into a civil war (Perthes 1994: p. 132; Picard 1996: pp. 89–103).[8]

Confessionalism in the post-civil war period

The first step on the way to ending the civil war was the accord of Ta'if, which laid out the new power balance in Lebanon and particularly paid tribute to Syria's dominant position by stating that Lebanon "maintains special relations with Syria which derive their strength from neighborhood, history and common brother-like interests" (Ta'if: IV).[9] The constitutional supremacy of the Maronites was finally and formally abolished and replaced by what has been called the rule of "three presidents" or the *Troika*. In this new arrangement, the Maronite President of the Republic, the Sunni Prime Minister, and the Shi'i Speaker of the House were all placed at the same level of power. According to the new Constitution, none of the three leaders is able to unseat either of the other two. Also, the ratio between Christians and Muslims in the parliament was changed to an equal proportion.[10]

Ta'if, the name of the place in Saudi Arabia where the accord was hammered out in October 1989, is accidentally based on the same root as the Arab word for "confession, denomination" *(ta'ifa)* (from which is derived *ta'ifiya*, "confessionalism"): surely a case of *nomen est omen*. The Ta'if accord (parts of its text are incorporated into the preamble and various articles of the 1990 Constitution) takes an ambiguous stance on the question of confessionalism. It expresses on the one hand an avowed commitment to a gradual and careful deconfessionalization of the political system in Lebanon and on the other proposes certain steps to abolish it. For example, the accord eliminates sectarian criteria for the recruitment of public servants, except for posts at the highest levels (I, 2, G, 1). It also abrogates the practice of stating the person's confession on identity cards (I, 2, G, 2). But besides these minor changes, Ta'if retains the old 1943 model. Article (J) of the preamble to the Constitution (almost identical to Ta'if I, 1, J) that states that "Any authority which contravenes the principle of coexistence is illegal" reminds one strikingly of the Article 16 of the "Declaration of the Rights of Man and the Citizen" of 1789.[11] Confessionalism is thus elevated to a primary constitutional good.

On the whole, the parallels to the Constitution of 1926 and the National Pact of 1943 are too obvious to call Ta'if a major break. Article

95 of the first Constitution in 1926 saw to a confessional representation in public employment only as a "temporary" measure in order to guarantee a "just" distribution among the confessions. The Ta'if accord and the Constitution of 1990 express once again in no uncertain terms their wish to abolish confessionalism. To that end, an institution would have to be installed by the parliament that would consider ways to achieve deconfessionalization.[12] Yet, "While proclaiming political deconfessionalization as a national objective, Ta'if entrusts the achievement of this goal to the confessional establishment. [...] It gives the confessional establishment an unguided, nonbinding, open-ended mandate to abolish itself" (Khairallah 1994: pp. 262f; Salam 1994: pp. 146ff).

The new Constitution seeks to restrict the powers of the confessional leaders, but at the same time affirms their predominant position. Thus, for example, Article 19 of the new Constitution creates a Constitutional Council "for the control of the constitutionality of laws and to resolve litigation and disputes arising from presidential and parliamentary elections." The same article gives the right of recourse to this Council not only "to the President of the Republic, to the President of the Chamber of Deputies, and to the President of the Council of Ministers, or to ten members of the Chamber of Deputies," but also to the "the heads of the legally recognized communities exclusively in what concerns personal status, liberty of conscience, exercise of the cult, and freedom of religious education." As matters stand today, then, the political system in Lebanon is still "confessionalism:" that is a form of religious consociationalism.

Staying on the same path or finding an exit?

Still on the agenda of Lebanese politics is the question of whether to continue on the trodden path of confessionalism or to find an exit door towards a fundamentally secularized state and society. Amongst the more or less outspoken defenders of confessionalism one may identify two currents. The first is that of muddling through with more or less honest intentions. Its representatives are often to be found among those whose power basis stems from a prominent role in the civil war period of 1975–90.[13] The second group of pro-confessionalists are those who plead for a benevolent and chastened confessionalism. According to their reasoning, one has to cut out from the confessionalist system the malicious and infested parts such as clientelism. To heal the body politic one has to remember the heritage of Muslim–Christian coexistence and to accept the peculiarity of each community's culture which flows into a common Lebanese culture.[14] What has to be striven for is a balance between the confessional affiliation and the public spirit as a citizen. This stance was propagated in the middle of the 1990s in an exemplary way by the multi-confessional committee "Permanent Council for Lebanese Dialog" *(al-mu'tamar ad-da'im li-l-hiwar al-lubnani)*, manned by prominent representatives of various confessions (Samir Frangié, Sa'ud al-Mawla, Muhammad as-Sammak, Muhammad Shamsaddin). In a joint declaration in 1995, published in the form of a pamphlet, the council said that both democracy and patriotism *(wataniya)* are based on the pluri-confessional structure of Lebanon and that neither can replace it. What is needed is simply the "Lebanonization" of the *tawa'if* (i.e. the confessional groups). Here, the aim of national unity is stressed, rather than the quest for a democratic political system: in other words, the democratic commitment of some of these positions is unclear.

The proponents of deconfessionalization are also not a monolithic group. They fall mainly into two groups. The first group (a prominent name in this group is Selim el-Hoss, who several times has held the post of Prime Minister) argues for a *political* deconfessionalization, as is also stipulated in the Ta'if accord (I, 2, G; see also above). Deconfessionalization would thus concern only matters in the national political arena, while personal status law would be left to the rule of the respective confessional groups. The major objection to the idea of "political" deconfessionalization, however, is that the proposed separation between a confessional and a non-confessional zone would not work. Laws and institutions in the confessional realm would easily breed a sectarian culture in all other areas of the body politic. Hence, the second group in this camp advocates a complete secularization of the political system and society.

But deliberations on these questions resemble the problem of troop disentanglement where all parties involved will only trust the process if the retreat of all parties can be at every moment verified and if it is on a strictly mutual basis. Particularly the Maronites fear that if only the first of these two processes is carried out, that is if there is political deconfessionalization without secularization, then the demographically dominant Muslims will impose their political visions. The call for political deconfessionalization-cum-secularization is therefore a more or less Christian position and thus easily falls prey to the traditional game of confessional power bargaining ("we give you political deconfessionalization if you give us secularization").

An assessment

The debate on confessionalism in Lebanon should take into account the following two factors. First, the overall power relations dominating Lebanon are of decisive importance. Lebanon since the beginning of the 1990s has been under strong Syrian influence. The common interpretation is that Syria is not interested in a deconfessionalized and secularized Lebanon. Confessionalism makes it easier for Syria to play off the Muslims against the Christians, that is to pursue a strategy of divide-and-rule. The other theory is that the Syrian regime had already realized the long-term impossibility of relying on the fragile confessionally segmented rule of the Alawis, and that Syria is therefore interested in a slow process of deconfessionalization also in Lebanon. Be that as it may, Lebanese deconfessionalization will depend on Syria's future political development.

Secondly, confessionalism intrudes in many respects into law. One important realm that it influences is the law of citizenship. Uri Davis, for example, goes so far as to argue (1997: p. 150) that the Constitution of 1926 (being modeled on the French constitution of 1871, and also drawing on the royalistic-restorative Belgian constitutions of 1831 and the Egyptian constitution of 1923), and its successor drafted in 1990, apply the principle of *jus sanguinis*. The most prominent and obvious case is that of the Palestinian refugees (with the exception of its Christian segment) who are not integrated into the Lebanese state.[15] Naturalization is a highly delicate question. In 1994, 100,000 persons were naturalized according to a confessional parity: Muslims from the frontier region near Israel (who had not been registered before as Lebanese citizens) and Christian immigrants who had come from various Arab states in the 1960s (Davis 1997: p. 153).

The most visible result of confessionalism in this context is the removal of personal status law and education from the realm of the state. Confessionalism clearly works here (intentionally or unintentionally) with a "split consciousness." The elites and leaders of the confessional groups demand that personal status law and education stay outside of the reach of the state, arguing that the respective groups' "individuality" must be respected and protected. At the same time, the confessional elites, now declaring themselves to be representatives of political interest groups, demand "democratic" participation in state legislation and the executive, and thus usurp areas that are clearly beyond the "personal-confessional" realm. Hence, the duality in the power structure and the consequent tension between the religious institutions on one hand, and the central government on the other, has been a major obstacle in the way of modernization and the implementation of the tenets of democracy with regard to the rights of individual citizens. This can best be seen in the debate on civil marriage.

President Hrawi's optional civil marriage proposal (1998)

In Lebanon, religious heads hold the political power. The Friday mosque *khutba* (sermon) is typically a political speech instructing the believers on how to respond to political events. It is the same with the Maronites. The Maronite Patriarch states his opinion on the political events of the week and criticizes the actions of the Cabinet and the President of the Republic in his Sunday sermons. Conflict arises every time the state tries to centralize its power and move away from sectarian influence. The proposal of President Elias Hrawi to introduce an optional civil marriage is a case in point.

So far, citizens in Lebanon have had to comply with religious laws concerning their birth, death, marriage, divorce, and inheritance. Currently, while granted the right to have a religious marriage, Lebanese citizens are not allowed to have a civil marriage. As every sect has its own distinct religious laws that regulate personal status and marriage, Lebanese people tend to marry mainly within the same sect. Muslim religious leaders, for example, have historically banned the marriage of a Muslim woman to a non-Muslim man. Moreover, religious laws do not allow for equality between men and women. The issue of civil marriage therefore carries tremendous political significance in Lebanon, and the prospect of introducing some form of civil marriage elicits much passion. Any suggestion of a civil marriage code threatens the religious heads' prerogatives within the judicial system. Furthermore, it potentially leads to the eradication of the closed sects through intermarriage.

Since its inception in 1920, Lebanon has witnessed four attempts to implement a civil code, and all efforts toward the attainment of this goal have failed (see Saadeh 2002: pp. 449–57). The latest proposal came from none other than the Maronite President of the Republic, Elias Hrawi, a few months prior to the end of his term in 1998. Significantly, President Hrawi's draft included an additional proposal demanding the abolition of sectarianism in politics. It was the timing of this bill that made many politicians suspicious of the real goals of this proposal. Opinion was divided, but many thought that the proposal was a clever maneuver on the part of the President to renew his term, something that the Constitution did not allow: by appearing as the champion of such a big cause, he would make himself indispensable for a new term in office (see, for example, *As-Safir* 31 March 1998: p. 2; *An-Nahar*, 1 April 1998: p. 2). Other politicians thought that, by trying to introduce civil marriage, the President was catering to the demands of the Christians who wanted either a sectarian state as

Lebanon stands now, or complete secularization in state and society. The Muslims retorted by demanding an eradication of sectarianism solely in the political realm. A non-sectarian representation in parliament would mean the triumph of Muslims due to their numerical superiority. In order to keep that superiority, religious law would continue to rule society in conformity with the tenets of Islam as expounded by the various religious *ulama*.

The civil marriage proposal of President Elias Hrawi has shown once again that, in a crisis situation, statesmen follow the interest of their sects, bringing the country to the brink of fragmentation.[16] The optional civil marriage was utterly rejected by the religious dignitaries because they perceived the proposal to be a first step in stripping them of their power over society.[17] This can be seen in the following account of the reactions of the three main sects that currently dominate the political scene.

The Sunni reaction

Sunni religious leaders have always opposed government attempts to legislate a civil status law in Lebanon. There are several reasons for this. One explanation is the identification of the Sunnis with the Muslim (Ottoman) Empire, where they were the rulers, and their yearning to return to that state of affairs. Another is that, after the breakdown of the Ottoman Empire, many of its institutions were preserved in Lebanon. Notably, the Sunni law courts kept their status as part and parcel of the governmental institutions, although Lebanon was labeled a "republic." As indicated above, the Constitution of the Lebanese Republic drafted in 1943 was modeled after the French example. It stipulated the separation of the state from religious matters, and the approval of the civil law by the people or their representatives, not by religious heads. Yet the *muftis* (local Islamic officials) still receive their monthly salaries from the Lebanese government like any other governmental official, and all of their rulings are published in the *Official Newsletter* as governmental decisions.

On 18 March 1998, President Elias Hrawi, who was chairing the meeting of the Cabinet, asked the ministers to vote on his previously circulated proposal for an optional civil marriage. Twenty-one ministers, both Christian and Muslim, voted in favor, while nine Christian and Muslim ministers voted against. The ministers who voted against the proposal were in the parliamentary bloc of Prime Minister Rafik Hariri (a Sunni Muslim). The Prime Minister saw in the proposal a weakening of the power of the Sunnis and refused to sign it. The Prime

Minister's rejection of the bill constituted a violation of the Constitution, because an overwhelming majority of the ministers had supported it and, according to the Constitution, the Prime Minister had to submit to a two-thirds majority vote in the cabinet. Faced with mounting pressure, he resorted to mobilizing popular opposition to the President (*An-Nahar* 21 March 1998).

To that end, the Prime Minister called the *mufti* of Lebanon, Muhammad Rashid Qabbani, who was on a visit to Saudi Arabia and asked him to return immediately to Beirut and stage demonstrations to protest the proposal. The *mufti* arrived the following day, on 19 March. Remarkably, the Sunni deputies in the parliament without a single exception united behind the Sunni *mufti* against other representatives of other confessional denominations in the same parliament, demonstrating once more that sectarian solidarity is more important than national unity. During the following months, the Sunni religious heads fought relentlessly against the optional civil marriage bill until it was ultimately withdrawn.

Actually, the Sunni opposition to the optional civil marriage started even before a vote was taken in the ministerial Cabinet. The head of the Sunni court, Mufid Shalaq, attacked the draft by stating: "This is a proposal that is directed against Islam. It aims to paralyze the role of the religious courts. In addition, it incites Moslems to renege on their faith." Further, Shalaq asked the government to stop registering civil marriages contracted abroad. He even threatened to force a divorce on all Muslim women who are married outside of their religion. Both the *mufti* of Mount Lebanon, Muhammad Ali al-Juzu, and the *mufti* of the Beqa' valley, *shaykh* Khalil al-Mays, adopted the same attitude (*An-Nahar* 26 January 1998: p. 6).

The bastion of resistance to the plan was the city of Tripoli, known as the incubus of radical Sunni movements such as the *Jama'ah al-Islamiyyah* and the *Tawhid* movement. Thus, the *mufti* of Tripoli summoned a meeting, which the overwhelming majority of the Sunni deputies of North Lebanon attended. The meeting interpreted the proposal as a step toward the abolition of religion and the spread of atheism. The deputies called for the immediate resignation of President Hrawi on the grounds that he had insulted the feelings of the Muslims. Both the "Committee for Muslim Salvation" and the *Jama'ah al-Islamiyyah* denounced the President's action as a precursor to civil war, and branded it unconstitutional. Beirut's Sunni societies and organizations concurred with this stand, and called for demonstrations in all the mosques of Lebanon. The *mufti* organized a mass demonstration in the Great Mosque of Tripoli, where thousands gathered and raised copies of the Qur'an, chanting (in reference to the Jewish tribe that was defeated by the Prophet Muhammad in Medina) "Khaybar, khaybar, the army of the Prophet Muhammad shall return." A delegation of the *Jama'ah al-Islamiyyah* proceeded to Damascus and met with the Deputy President of Syria, Abdul-Halim Khaddam. The latter urged the withdrawal of Hrawi's proposal (*An-Nahar* 25 March 1998: p. 6). Demonstrations spread to the capital and took place on a daily basis, threatening civil unrest and insurrection. Although the government had banned demonstrations in the famous 1994 "censorship laws,"[18] it stood by and did not dare to interfere.

Thus, the Sunni religious leaders condemned the civil marriage proposal by arguing that the private affairs of citizens have been and will always be the domain of the religious institutions.[19] *Mufti* Muhammad Rashid Qabbani saw civil marriage "as a Western invention that brings the disintegration of family and society. Moreover, it leads to atheism." Qabbani also argued that "civil marriage is part of a plot to initiate secularism in Lebanon, so as to spread this virus to the rest of the Arab world." The *Tawhid* movement, the *Jama'ah al-Islamiyyah*, the *Committee for Islamic Unity*, the *Islamic Pious Society*, the *Moslem Youth*, the *Moslem Consolation Committee*, and the Sunni branch of the Scouts stated that a civil code would make people obey man-made laws rather than laws sent by God. Every Muslim who was tempted to contract a civil marriage would immediately be labeled a *kafir* (heretic) (*An-Nahar* 28 February 1998, 23–30 March 1998).

The Shi'ite reaction

At first, the Shi'i religious dignitaries did not react to the approval of the optional civil marriage by the Cabinet of ministers. The Sunni *mufti,* Muhammad Rashid Qabbani, summoned the head of the Shi'i Higher Council, Muhammad Mahdi Shamsaddin, who had always opposed the establishment of a secular state and of civil marriage and had previously made the following statement: "This law threatens to undermine Muslim and Christian religious courts and infringes on people's private lives. Lebanese citizens cannot be ruled by a law common to all sects" (*The Daily Star* 8 January 1998: p. 4). The outcome of their meeting was a joint statement denouncing the government's proposal. Shaykh Shamsaddin had also reiterated that neither the government nor the parliament had the right to discuss the issue of civil marriage. The Shi'i Legislative Committee concurred with Shamsaddin that the rules concerning private lives are the prerogatives of the religious heads of all denominations (*As-Safir* 25 March 1998).

Shaykh Shamsaddin sees life in Lebanon as divided into two distinct spheres: the political sphere that concerns the state and the private sphere that concerns only the religious dignitaries. In one of his *khutbas*, he explicitly elaborates this point: "The role of the secular parties is to be involved in politics, the electoral laws, the organization of the bureaucracy and the implementation of taxes. But parties have no right to meddle with marriage, divorce and inheritance laws" (quoted in *An-Nahar* 21 March 1998: p. 6). Although this stand appears more tolerant than that of the Sunnis, it still refuses to allow citizens the choice of an "optional" civil marriage. Yet none of the Shi'i religious leaders went as far as the Sunni *mufti* Muhammad Rashid Qabbani to proclaim a *kafir* to whomsoever contracts a civil marriage.

Moreover, the Shi'i camp did not take a homogeneous stand like the Sunnis. Hezbollah and Amal movements, for example, took opposite stands. While Hezbollah attacked the proposal, the head of the Amal movement and Speaker of the House, Nabih Berri, approved it, as evidenced in the fact that the Shi'ite Cabinet ministers associated with the Amal movement voted in favor of the proposal. The head of Hezbollah, Muhammad Hasan Nusrallah, and the deputies representing Hezbollah in the parliament, known as *Kutlat al-Wafa' lil-Muqawamah* (Loyalty to the Resistance Bloc), denounced the proposal, with deputy Ibrahim Amin al-Sayyid considering civil marriage as an implementation of atheism. As for the prominent Hezbollah leader, Muhammad Husayn Fadlallah, he made it clear that any Moslem who contracts a civil marriage will be considered an adulterer/adulteress (*An-Nahar* 20–27 March 1998).

Thus, on the Shi'i side there was a cleavage between the religious heads on one hand, and the politicians and intellectuals on the other. While the former rejected the optional civil marriage bill, the latter were in favor. The Shi'i deputy and former Speaker of the House, Husayn al-Husayni, for example, accused the religious leadership of manipulating the sects. He stressed that Lebanon is not a theocratic state and that the sects have to recognize the supremacy of the state and individual rights. Only one religious Shi'i figure defied the other Shi'i religious heads as well as the point of view of both Christian and Muslim religious leaders. Shaykh Muhammad Hasan al-Amin insisted on the necessity of establishing a secular state because, he said, sectarianism has been a stumbling block towards progress in Lebanon (*An-Nahar* 11 March 1998, 21 March 1998).

The Maronite position

Among Christians, the Maronites took the lead in attacking the civil marriage proposal. The Maronite Patriarch, Mar Nusrallah Butrus

Sfayr, denounced it, as did a number of Maronite politicians. The reason for this was the fact that Christians became a minority at the end of the civil war, due to emigration in large numbers. While still a majority prior to the civil war, the Christians favored secularism; but now the tables were turned. This view was clearly expressed by the former President of the Maronite Union, Ernest Karam: "President Hrawi has connected the issue of civil marriage with that of the abolition of sectarianism in politics. We believe this act to be extremely dangerous as it violates the principle of power sharing between the sects" (*An-Nahar* 21 March 1998: p. 6). Thus, from the Maronite point of view, abolition of confessionalism would mean the triumph of Islam, because the latter is in the numerical majority.

The Maronite Patriarch's stand was very close to that of the Sunni *mufti*, Muhammad Rashid Qabbani. Similarly intolerant, he decreed that anyone who dares to contract a civil marriage will be denied the last sacrament. Since the draft proposal for the "optional" civil marriage also included a clause that would abolish sectarian representation in politics, both Christians and Sunni Muslims felt threatened by the Shi'ite majority that would eventually dominate the political scene if the power-sharing arrangement between the various confessional groups at the governmental level were ended. However, while the position of the Sunni *mufti* was in harmony with the (Sunni) Prime Minister Rafik Hariri, the attitude of the Maronite Patriarch clashed with that of the (Maronite) President, who in turn was upset because the Patriarch's stand led to a considerable weakening of his own position and proposal. Consequently, several Christian organizations, such as the Lebanese Forces, the Christian Democratic Union, and the Human Rights Movement in Lebanon, condemned a proposal that would include the abolition of sectarianism in politics along with an optional civil marriage (*An-Nahar* 31 March 1998: p. 4).

By contrast, the Greek Orthodox Bishop George Khodr saw the reactions of both the Sunnis and Maronites as a refusal to separate Church from State. According to him, such a stand had stopped all creativity and evolution in the country. Bishop Khodr's position was in tune with the majority of the Greek Orthodox, who actually favor a secular state and society and divesting religion of all temporal powers, and was confirmed by the reactions of the Greek Orthodox deputies. The National Bloc Party, on the other hand, although a pioneer in the 1950s in its demand for secularism under the leadership of Raymond Edde, changed its position fifty years later and decided that the time was not ripe to discuss such a project, although some of its members still backed the introduction of civil marriage (*An-Nahar* 28 March

1998). Again, this attitude reflected the fear of Muslim hegemony, as the National Bloc is strictly a Christian party.

Finding gaps in the new Constitution

The political rift following the proposal exposed the gaps that plague the Constitution as signed in 1989 at Ta'if. In case of a stalemate between the president and the prime minister, there is no available mechanism to resolve the problem. This is due to the fact that many prerogatives were stripped from the presidency at a time when Syria mistrusted the Maronites because one of their parties, the "Lebanese Forces," sided openly with, and got arms from, Israel. Henceforth, the president could no longer dismiss his prime minister. In addition, the president was no longer the head of the executive branch of the government, and the ministerial cabinet became an independent institution that could be dismissed only by a two-thirds majority of the parliament. But the latter is a highly unlikely prospect simply because the cabinet ministers are chosen from among the deputies and in conformity with the "Grand Coalition" of the most important sects in the country.

Another flaw pertains to the ministerial cabinet itself, for nothing in the Constitution indicates what course to follow in case the prime minister refuses to sign a bill passed by an overwhelming majority of the cabinet. In the instance narrated above, two problems became apparent, originating from the ambiguity of Articles 54 and 56 of the Constitution. One, while the Constitution places a five-day time limit on the president to sign a draft bill to be sent to the legislative branch for approval, it places no such time limit on the prime minister. Two, the Constitution does not specify what course of action to follow when the prime minister refuses to sign a bill, while, if the president fails to sign a bill within the specified time limit, it passes automatically to the parliament.

The proposal turned into a showdown between the Maronite President of the Republic and the Sunni Prime Minister. This was, in reality, part of a bigger conflict between the sects and the attempt of each one to gain power at the expense of the other. The Maronite President of the Republic, Elias Hrawi, however, had resorted to a shrewd move by allying himself with the Shi'i Speaker of the House, Nabih Berri, against the Sunni Prime Minister, Rafik Hariri. Knowing that his proposal of an optional civil marriage would be defeated in the cabinet by the votes of both the ministers appointed by Hariri and those appointed by Berri, President Hrawi had added to his draft an additional proposal demanding the abolition of sectarianism in politics: a demand that was repeatedly made by Nabih Berri. Having thus neutralized the Shi'is, the Maronite President was able to secure a majority over the Sunni Prime Minister.

Still, the votes in the cabinet did not follow an absolute sectarian division. The ministers were divided in accordance with their allegiance to one of the three "presidents," each of whom had the right to appoint ministers to the Cabinet. Thus, for example, the Greek Orthodox Bishara Merhej, known to be a secular person and a member of the Parliamentary Committee for Human Rights, voted against the proposal because he was selected by the Sunni Prime Minister, Rafik Hariri, to be in his Cabinet. But, Faruq al-Barbir, who heads the Sunni Maqasid hospital, and Ghazi Sayf al-Din, another Sunni, who heads the Ba'th party, voted for the proposal because the Syrian government was also in favor of it. By contrast, Basim al-Sab', a Shi'i who is politically against the Shi'ite Speaker of the House, Nabih Berri, and a member of the Hariri Bloc, refused to sign the proposal.

The survey of the reactions to Hrawi's optional civil marriage reveals that secularists were marginalized because of the confessional structure of the state. The Constitution of Lebanon does not conceptually allow any category of citizen other than the one identified by religion. Secularists are unable to find representation within state institutions and can only express themselves from outside of the state structure. Consequently, any attempts that were made came as isolated instances from either students or non-governmental institutions. For example, in April, over 12,000 students signed a petition demanding the implementation of civil marriage. Representatives of the Syrian Social Nationalist Party, the Socialist Progressive Party of Walid Junblat, the Free Nationalists (followers of General Michel Aoun), some members of the National Bloc, the Secular Democratic Party, the Workers' Union, the Rights of People movement, the Committee for Women's Rights, the Cultural Council for Southern Lebanon, and the Lebanese Human Rights Society signed another petition in a joint meeting. In addition, student delegations visited President Hrawi, expressing support for his project. Even in Nabatiyya (South Lebanon), an area that is supposed to be a stronghold of the Hezbollah movement, 26 lawyers managed to sign a petition demanding the implementation of an optional civil marriage. These lawyers stated that citizens should be granted the freedom to choose in accordance with the bill of Human Rights (*As-Safir* 31 March 1998).[20]

Thus, although the government is run by a coalition of the major religious sects, there have always been secular parties and social movements that have rejected this state of affairs and demanded the eradication of confessionalism in the political and judicial realms. Hence, society is not only divided along sectarian lines, despite the fact that these vertical lines are the dominant ones, but it also exhibits a rift between those who believe in secularism and those who resist such change. Unfortunately, one of the main safety valves of the sectarian system has been the emigration of a sizable number of those professionals who reject confessionalism. Without sectarian backing, they are unable to locate jobs solely on their own merit.

Conclusion

Lebanon's political structure revolves around the antagonistic and incongruous axis of religious authority versus state authority. This raises the question of whether Lebanon can rightly be called a democratic state, for it clearly seems to violate the very principles upon which democracy is built, namely "equality before the law" and "equal political participation." The principle of "equality before the law" necessitates the existence of one law for all citizens. Lebanon, however, has 18 sets of laws that regulate individuals' personal lives, leading to the unequal treatment of citizens. In Lebanon, "liberal citizenship" (i.e. the bundle of rights necessary for individual freedom), is hampered and restricted by confessionalism and by a patrimonial residue in personal status law. Hence, the Charter of Human Rights signed by Lebanon is utterly disregarded as to the freedom of creed and belief. The principle of "equal political participation" is also violated, because only Christian and Muslim candidates are allowed to run for parliamentary elections. Secularists are barred from expressing themselves politically and hence denied their rights as citizens. Thus, "political citizenship," which guarantees participation in the exercise of political power, is also violated by the power monopoly of the confessional elites.

Notes

* The sections of this chapter on "confessionalism" were mostly written by the first author and the sections on "civil marriage" by the second author.

1 In 1995, the Copts were admitted as the eighteenth community. The prominent, and hence the politically empowered, sects are the Maronites, Sunnis, Shi'is, Greek Orthodox, Greek Catholic, and the Druze.

2 Arend Lijphart (1977: pp. 3–4). Lijphart states that he coined the term "consociationalism" by drawing on Johannes Althusius's concept of *consociatio* (community of common destiny, cooperative).

3 For more details, see Sofia Saadeh (1993). Alongside the term "confessionalism"

one can find a number of other terms that designate more or less the same but show varying degrees of sympathy toward the institutions and practice of confessionalism: "consociationalism" (Antoine N. Messarra, Theodor Hanf), "political communitarianism" (Elizabeth Picard), "sectopolitics" (Nazih Richani) or "sectarianism" (Ussama Makdisi). Many thinkers have hailed the confessional system as being the best regime for Lebanon. See, for example, Kamal al-Hajj (1961: p. 12, p. 40, p. 196).

4 A prominent proponent of this line of argumentation is Antoine Messarra (1986: p. 107, 1994: p. 21, 1997: p. 152).

5 Some opponents of confessionalism also stress the insurmountability of the deep-rooted confessionalism and therefore equally tend to mystify it. See, for example, Ussama Makdisi (2000: p. 174).

6 Edmond Rabbath (1973: p. 517) characterizes Article 95 as the major stepping stone on the road to a pathological development of political confessionalism.

7 Elizabeth Picard (1996: p. 7). Picard therefore rejects Lijphart's argument that Lebanon is a democracy by consensus comparable to the Dutch or Swiss systems.

8 Gerhard Lehmbruch (1967: p. 55), almost a decade before the outbreak of the civil war, expressed skepticism about Lebanon's fate and stated that, also in countries with a far more progressed industrialization, the political culture of *amibilis compositio* tends to spill over into all other areas of political decision-making.

9 For the Ta'if Accord of 1989 and the Constitution of 1990, see Béchara Ménassa (1995).

10 Modification to Article 24 of the Constitution by Ta'if I, 2A, 5 states: "Until the Chamber of Deputies adopts an electoral law without confessional community apportionment, parliamentary seats will be allotted according to the following rules: A. Equally between Christians and Muslims ... ." Here, "Christian" refers to the combination of all the Christian sects (Maronites, Orthodox, Protestant, etc.) and "Muslim" the combination of all the Muslim sects (Sunni, Shiite, Druze), despite the rivalry between the sects in each group.

11 "A society in which the observance of the law is not assured, nor the separation of powers defined, has no constitution at all."

12 "The abolition of the political confessional system is an essential national aim which must be achieved by means of a step-by-step plan. The Chamber of Deputies, elected on the basis of the apportionment in equal halves between Muslims and Christians, must take adequate steps to achieve this objective and form a national committee under the presidency of the President of the Republic bringing together, with the President of the Chamber and the President of the Council of Ministers, personalities drawn from the politicians, intellectuals, and leading members of society. The assignment of the Committee will consist of studying and proposing methods capable of abolishing the confessional system (...)" (Ta'if I, 2, G). Corresponding phrases are given in Preamble (H) and Article 95 of the constitution.

13 For example, Nabih Berri, Speaker of Parliament (and, as such, a member of the *Troika*) and leader of the Shi'ite Amal movement since the 1980s, confirmed in 1995 his practice to appoint Shi'ites to positions within his reach as long as the confessionalist system had a firm hold on Lebanon and as long as Maronites, Sunnies, and other sects would comply with the system. Berri justified his practice with the hypocritical argument that he wanted to illustrate by his confessionalist policy the dangers of confessionalism (see *An-Nahar*, 28 February 1995: p. 3).

14 See, for example, the discussion between Ghassan Tueni, editor of the liberal Beirut

newspaper *An-Nahar* and a devoted anti-confessionalist, and the Maronite Bishop Ra'y, where both could agree on this point (*An-Nahar*, 6 February 1995: p. 4).

15 Article I of the preamble to the Constitution of 1990 states: "The Lebanese territory is a unified territory for all Lebanese. Every Lebanese has the right to reside in any part of this territory and to profit from it, under the sovereignty of the law, without division of the people on the base of any allegiance whatsoever, and without dismemberment, partition or implantation." This last term refers to a possible mass integration of Palestinians into the Lebanese system.

16 See Muhammad Muqallid, "Qanun al-ahwal al-shakhsiyyah" (*An-Nahar* 20 March 1998: p. 19), who criticizes both the Muslim religious leaders who behave as the "representatives of God on earth," though this is not an injunction of the Qur'an, and the behavior of the deputies and ministers who act not as defenders of the state, but rather as followers of the religious heads.

17 President Hrawi's proposal was rather traditional in outlook. Regarding the question of the custody of children for example, it followed the tenets of Muslim law. It stated that the father has full custody over his children in the case of divorce. However, even this conservative proposal clashed with Muslim law in two major respects. The Presidential proposal banned polygamy and, more importantly, it allowed Muslim women to marry non-Muslims. It is this latter point that the Sunnis opposed the more (see *An-Nahar* 6 February 1998: p. 6).

18 On the censorship laws, see "Qanun al-Matbu'at wal-Uqubat" (*An-Nahar* 5 February 1994: p. 3) and Sofia Saadeh (1999: pp. 151–8).

19 For the *khutba* of the *mufti* of Mount Lebanon, Muhammad Ali al-Juzu, see *An-Nahar* (21 March 1998: p. 6). The late head of the Shi'ite Higher Council, Muhammad Mahdi Shamsaddin, had made a similar statemen, a year earlier; see *The Daily Star* (5 November 1997: p. 4).

20 Often, however, fanatic elements dominated the scene and disrupted attempts to discuss this issue in a rational manner. For instance, when the Political Science Department at the American University of Beirut organized a panel discussion on the proposal, fundamentalists interrupted the panelists with screams of "*Allahu Akbar*" (God is Great). The authorities were afraid to intervene and restore order. As a result, the panel discussion had to be suspended, fearing an eruption of violence.

7 The rise and fall of civil society in Iraq

Sami Zubaida

It is commonly stated that the Iraqi population is divided into Sunnis in the center, Shi'is in the south, and Kurds in the north, and that this division constitutes the main basis of political solidarity and affiliation, to the extent of endangering the unity of the country. Those who know the country well will recognize this conventional wisdom as a caricature. True, these are important lines of division, and certain Kurdish forces have a long history of nationalist struggle, yet this view hides many differences that cut across these lines. Above all, it obscures the formation of a modern civil society and political and cultural fields in the country over the course of the twentieth century, fields which involved the active participation of members of all communities, not on bases of communal solidarity but of political and ideological commitments. It is the suppression of these political divisions under successive governments and their near elimination under the Ba'thist regime that enhances the salience of particularistic solidarities.

I use "civil society" in a specific sense: it is the society of citizens, active agents in a public space, informed and involved in associations and parties, in contests and debates.[1] In societies emerging into modernity in the nineteenth and twentieth centuries, whether from an imperial or colonial past, it was the formation of the modern state which established the conditions and the spaces for civil society. This was the world of government functionaries, intellectuals, teachers, journalists, and artists, as well as modern sectors of business and the professions, in some instances extending to sectors of the "common people" such as organized elements of modern working classes. At first, these strata coexisted with "traditional" sectors which constituted the majority of populations, sectors which were still governed by the organization and sentiments of community, whether of tribe, religion, ethnicity, village, or region, as well as groupings of bazaar, guilds, and patronage networks. The intelligentsia of civil society were, of course, drawn from these sectors and bore the traces of their origins, but, nevertheless, formed styles of life, outlooks, and loyalties shaped by the modern political and ideological fields. Equally, the "traditional" sectors were transformed by the processes of capitalism and modernity, but reconstituted elements of original loyalties and sentiments in relation to the modern state and its economic fields. The members of "tribes," for instance, were dispersed into different locations, many of them urbanized, yet constituted networks of solidarity and mutual aid within new, modern situations. These different elements were represented in the state and the political fields, with cross-cutting and contradictory currents of ideology and communal interest.

Iraqi nationalism

Before proceeding with the argument in relation to modern Iraq, let me sketch the history of the country in the twentieth century.[2] Iraq was formed as a modern state under British Mandate in 1920. Its constituents were the Ottoman *vilayets* (provinces) of Baghdad, Basra, and Mosul. It was the product of two colonial administrations: first of the modernizing Ottoman state of the Tanzimat and the Young Turks' Constitution of 1908, then of the British Mandate. The Shi'ite shrine cities of Najaf and Karbala, as well as the Shi'ite centers of Baghdad, had close connections with Iran and its religious institutions. As such, their *ulama* and notables participated in the events of the Iranian Constitutional Revolution of 1906. Sectors of the Iraqi intelligentsia and *ulama*, therefore, were exposed to modern political ideas and vocabularies on a number of fronts, parts of different political worlds: the Ottoman, the Iranian, British Colonial, and finally the "Arab Revolt" of World War I. This last produced the Hashemite dynasty of Hijaz as British clients, and one of their princes, Faysal, would be made King of the new Arab state of Iraq under British Mandate in 1921. This was in the wake of a rebellion against British occupation in 1920, celebrated by Iraqi and Arab nationalists as *thawrat al-'ishrin*, the 1920 Revolution. In fact, it was a coalition of different groups and interests: tribes jealous of their independence as well as pursuing opportunities for pillage, Ottoman officials out of a job, and some Shi'i *ulama* suspicious of European incursions on their culture and power. What is important, however, is that their leaders spoke in terms of the modern political vocabularies of nation, representation, and constitutions. Iraq did acquire its independence and membership of the League of Nations in 1932, but firmly under British influence, with a considerable British military presence.

The monarchical regime under British control, which lasted until 1958, was firmly Sunni and Arab, ruling over an Arab population, which is predominantly Shi'ite, and a Kurdish enclave in the north. This pattern dominated the politics of the Iraqi state. Opposition to British control was widespread, but from different and contradictory positions. The Sunni Arabs inclined towards pan-Arab nationalism, looking to a predominantly Sunni Arab world. The other main direction was that of the Left, mainly the Communist Party of Iraq (CPI) and later the National Democratic Party. These tended to "Iraqist" rather than pan-Arab nationalism, and attracted some Shi'ites, Christians, and Jews, as well as Kurds (who also had their own nationalist movements, at war with the Iraqi state for much of the twentieth century). Much of Iraqi politics was communalist, representing the interests and solidarities of tribes, regions, religious groups, and notable families, much like elsewhere in the region. However, ideological politics was superimposed on this scene, not just as a guise for communal politics, but with genuine commitment to nation and citizenship. These issues came to the fore after the first Iraqi revolution in 1958 which toppled the monarchy and British control (see Zubaida 1991: pp. 197–210).

The Qasim period (1958–63) loosened the communalist bonds of Sunni rule and its clients. Qasim himself was of mixed Sunni/Shi'i parentage and generally Iraqist in outlook, under attack from pan-Arabist Nasserites and Ba'thists. He brought modern intellectuals and technocrats, mostly of leftist and Iraqist outlook, into the circles of government. Although punctuated by putsches and conspiracies by opponents, and repressive campaigns by security forces, this period was, nevertheless, the most open and ideologically diverse in the modern history of Iraq. It was then that the power of the tribes, the clans, and the communities came under severest challenge with progressive policies, such as land reforms and legal reforms of family law, and from ideological politics. It was then, also, that the Communist Party succeeded in wide-ranging mobilization of many sectors of the population. This in turn provoked reactions from opposing forces, mostly brands of Arab nationalists. These movements were not confined to politics but reinforced the already-established cultural and artistic manifestations, from literature to theatre and the plastic arts, and an intense journalistic field to go with these. Wider sectors of the population were brought into the civil society of citizens. This political effervescence was, of course, to lead to severe and bloody conflicts in an unstable society. In these conflicts, the "traditional" forces came forth in ideological garb, mostly as Arab nationalists. And it was these that were eventually to overthrow Qasim, in 1963, and institute a clan-based military rule, which was to metamorphose into the present regime.

Qasim was overthrown by a Ba'thist *coup d'état* in 1963, reportedly with American backing, fearing the communist influence in the Qasim regime. It was then that the Ba'thists showed their flare for brutal repression when they engaged in wholesale massacres to undermine the popular bases of the defunct regime and of the CPI. They were to be displaced later that year by another military clique consisting of conservative nationalist and Islamic Sunni officers from Takrit and its neighbouring cities and constituent tribes, under the leadership of one General Arif (succeeded, after his accidental death, by a brother). This regime, lasting into 1968, was virulently sectarian and communalist, restoring Sunni ascendancy and reversing many of the previous reformist measures. In 1968, the Ba'thists returned to power with another *coup d'état*, and instituted another reign of terror. The communal and ideological composition of the new clique was initially mixed, with even some Shi'i figures in their ranks. However, the ascendant military personnel were Sunni officers from similar backgrounds to the previous regime. Saddam Hussein, not a military man, started his ascent to power at that point, and his ruthless methods involved successive purges of the army and the Ba'th Party, ultimately insuring the power of loyal cliques from his own region and tribe. The army, mostly officered by his loyalists, was firmly subordinated to political control, and the Ba'th Party, largely de-ideologized, became a vehicle of loyalty to the regime, penetrating and controlling all sectors of state and society. Saddam formally assumed the Presidency in 1979 and retained it until the recent war which overthrew him.

Civil society of citizens

Let us now return to the formation of civil society within that history. The modern state, journalism and "print capitalism," political parties, educational institutions, the professions, and modern sectors of business all produced their intelligentsia at least partly liberated from the bonds and horizons of kinship and primary loyalties, many with ideologically framed aspirations pertaining to the nation and its future. Reading the memoirs of public figures and literati of the early twentieth century, we find accounts of these groups, their journals and political ambitions, their venues of salons and cafés, their conspiracies and intrigues, and the conflicts that culminated in repression and violence. Different brands of nationalism: pan-Arabist and Iraqist, different ideologies, ranging from fascism to communism to liberal notions, all mingled and fought in various groupings, parties and clubs, now public, now clandestine, occasionally feeding into military conspiracies. The actors on this stage comprised Sunnis, Shi'is, Christians, Jews, and Kurds. Every actor was identified in terms of communal origins, and these identifications were at times important in the waging of contests, but these identifications, while influencing political alignments, did not determine them (Zubaida 2002: pp. 205–15).

From the point of view of the ruling cliques of the authoritarian states which invariably developed in the region, the ideological politics were threatening because they were aimed at reform and sometimes revolution. They also resorted to mass organization, threatening to bring sectors of the common people into the ideological politics of civil society. Such certainly was the threat of communist organization and mobilization from the 1940s. Ruling cliques, starting with British, were often happier making deals with tribes and communities to assure their loyalty and cooperation. In repeated conflicts with Kurdish nationalists, for instance, governments always resorted to "loyal" Kurdish tribes to fight on their behalf, loyalties which were often fickle and followed prevailing winds of power and interest. Religious opinion and confessional loyalties were often mobilized against the supposedly atheist communists. And of course, primordial loyalties of clan and patronage were often at the base of the ruling cliques themselves.

I should like at this point to narrate the tales of two different individuals, tales which will illustrate the departure of individuals from their communal rootedness and their relation to it: Muhammad Mahdi al-Jawahiri, the illustrious poet and publicist, and an obscure Jewish doctor I shall call Dr Naji. These biographies will illustrate the "imagination" of an Iraqi nation in the lives of constituent figures in the civil society of citizens that was forming in the first half of the twentieth century. Both, in different ways, felt and resisted the pull of communal identification. Jawahiri consciously rejected communal loyalty in favor of a public stance of citizenship and defense of the Iraqi nation. Naji, not overtly political, went through similar tensions and conflicts, but his stances as a citizen followed implicitly from his professional status and social location. The nationalist and Ba'th regimes which followed the overthrow of Qasim in the 1960s progressively restored communalism and tribalism, deliberately as support for their power, but also as a consequence of the repressive and clientelistic regimes they inaugurated.

Jawahiri

Jawahiri (1903–99) is renowned as much for his literary output as for his political activism.[3] He became closely identified with the Left, sympathetic to the Communist Party, celebrated or grieved the triumphs, defeats and martyrdom of popular struggles in his poetry, and suffered prison and exile on many occasions, to the last decades of his life spent in Prague, then Syria.

Jawahiri came from a family of Shi'ite *ulama* in the shrine city of Najaf. In the nineteenth and till the early decades of the twentieth centuries, Najaf and Karbala operated almost as autonomous city states under the rule of rival *mujtahids*, combined with control of their quarters by lineages and alliances between them.[4] Tribal *'asabiya* (solidarity) was the dominant social bond, maintaining boundaries, factions, and conflicts. Jawahiri was educated in the religious schools, which included extensive literary components, which were to attract the young student over to religion. In his late teens, his poetry found favor in the now national press, and his talent was noted. He soon found himself in Baghdad, and in 1927, through the patronage and connections of his influential uncle, was offered a job as a school teacher. It is at this point that the religious sectarianism comes into play.

Sati' al-Hussri, the Arab nationalist theorist, was Director of Education, and embarked on a program of Arab national revival through education. Within this framework, the Shi'a were suspect: association with Iran and with local and regional solidarities, separated from the rest of the Arab world by the boundary of religion. In Iraq, Arabism continued to be rooted, for the most part, as we saw, in the Sunni Arab population, while Shi'is and Kurds, if political, tended to the Left, which, in turn, formed the focus for Iraqist identification. Jawahiri fell foul of Hussri: the latter contended that Jawahiri was really Iranian (to Jawahiri's outrage at this Turk, who spoke Arabic with a thick accent, questioning his Arab identity). The job offer was withdrawn, and there followed a tussle between the token Shi'i Minister of Education and Sati' al-Hussri. In the meantime, also through his uncle's influence and the patronage of a Shi'i *alim* and notable in Baghdad, Jawahiri was introduced to King Faysal I, who liked the young man and appointed him to the Court Diwan (*diwan al-tashrifat*) alongside the sons of some illustrious families, where he served for three years. So far, the game is being played: Najafi *nasab* (lineage), as well as the young man's talents, bring him to high and promising office. Faysal was playing a balancing game, and among all the ex-Ottoman Sunnis, Syrians, and Hijazis, he made a token appointment of an Iraqi and a Shi'i.

Jawahiri, however, ruined his prospects by refusing to continue with the game. As part of his active and turbulent literary and journalistic life, Jawahiri was increasingly his own man, adopting critical and outspoken stances. In one of these, he turned against the loyalty of *nasab* and attacked prominent *ulama* of Najaf. These *ulama* had opposed the foundation of a girls' school in the shrine city, and Jawahiri published a poem *al-Raj'iyyun* (the reactionaries) a biting satire on the hypocrisy and venality of the *ulama*. It included the line: *wa minhum lususun, wa minhum lawatun wa-zanatu* ("and in their ranks there are thieves and pederasts and fornicators"). Predictably, this drew the ire of the notables, and a flood of protests to the King for sheltering such a person. This was the very constituency that the King tried to cultivate through appointing Jawahiri. This was the beginning of the end for the court career. Thereafter, Jawahiri was thrown onto the world of literature, journalism, and politics, all closely interwoven in that village-like public sphere of the incipient Iraqi nation. He soon developed a distinctive critical voice and a life of political adventure. Yet, under the monarchical regime (which ended in 1958), Jawahiri continued to draw on the patronage and influence of the political elite, including royal personalities. These were deeply ambivalent connections on both sides, yet it did procure him positions, grants, and mediations when he found himself in trouble and difficulty, which was often. After the 1958 revolution, Jawahiri was showered with honours and positions, but not for long. He soon fell out with General Qasim and ended up in exile. The Ba'thist regime's attempts to woo him back did not succeed.

Jawahiri, then, is a prominent illustration of the detachment and deracination of the individual from corporate allegiance, as part of the process of the formation and imagination of the nation. He developed his active citizenship in the context of the incipient locations and institutions of civil society and the public sphere: the press and publishing, political parties, clubs, cafés, and salons, and occasionally political prisons. His poetry was the poetry of public spaces, not only printed but declaimed in meetings, parties, and demonstrations, where the different sectors of an Iraqi public met and formed their opinion and imagination.

Many were to follow this path of citizenship and deracination from communal attachments and loyalties, though the roots within these communities may have left their traces. The Iraqi Left, and particularly the Communist Party, constituted a magnet for the renegades from all communities, who abandoned the bonds and securities of primary allegiance in favor of a political identification as citizen and patriot. Jawahiri spoke this sentiment in his famous line: *ana al-Iraqu, lisani qalbuhu, wa-dami furatuhu, wa-kiyani minhu ashtaru* ("I am Iraq, my tongue is her heart, my blood her Euphrates, my being from her branches formed").

Dr Naji

My second illustration, Dr Naji (1915–2002), is very different.[5] He was not political, and did not set out explicitly to challenge the traditional order or communal loyalties. He was explicitly faithful to his Jewish community, though not an observant Jew. However, his professional activity and the social locations to which it led him effectively cut him adrift from his communal moorings and into a socially promiscuous interaction with a wide range of Iraqis. As he declared at one point in an interview, he forgot that he was a Jew (see below). The fact that Dr Naji was a Jew is particularly significant for our narrative, because the Jews were subsequently considered by many Iraqis as well as Jews to have been a separate, even alien community, and as part of that wider Jewish belonging which became attached to Israel, and as such hostile to the Arabs. The story of Dr Naji illustrates the problems with this picture.

The Jews, being among the most educated and prosperous of Iraqis, constituted the major part of the urban middle class, especially of Baghdad, in the earlier decades of the twentieth century. Their business community and intelligentsia played a crucial part in the formation of the modern Iraqi state and society. Apart from their prominence in trade, finance, and industry, they also participated widely in the public sphere, as civil servants (many of high rank), lawyers, including prominent judges, teachers, and professors, journalists, editors and poets, and as medics. They were particularly prominent in the world of music, and many of the instrumentalists, singers, and composers of these years were Jews. The first Iraqi radio orchestra in 1936 was composed of mostly Jewish musicians (Kojaman 2001). They were aided in these spheres by the fact that, like the majority of Iraqis, their language was Arabic, though they were amongst the first to learn European languages. With the conflict between Arabs and Jewish settlers in Palestine, and the continuing significance of this issue for all Arabs, including Iraqis, the Jews were never "normal" citizens. The traditional communalist antagonisms were reinforced by the modern conflicts, and Jews suffered discrimination, and on occasion repression and violence. But despite that, many of them shared in the imagination of the Iraqi nation and the citizenship stance in the public sphere, as Naji's story will illustrate.

Naji (not his real name) was born in 1915, and qualified as a doctor in 1936. Thereafter, lacking the resources and connections to establish a private practice, he continued in government employment. In that, he also suffered from discrimination as a Jew and lacked the patronage necessary for a more favorable posting. He worked in rural and provincial posts until the end of the 1950s, when he retired to Baghdad and engaged in private practice. He remained there until 1970 when, after the 1968 Ba'thist coup, terror campaigns against many sectors of Iraqi society started with the Jews. Naji was imprisoned and maltreated, and eventually left Iraq with nearly all of the remaining Jews. I met and interviewed him in London in the late 1980s.

Naji did not deliberately detach himself from the religious community. His deracination was a cumulative process, conditioned by his physical separation from the centers of Jewish life, and his absorption into Iraqi provincial life. Although there were other Jewish doctors in a similar position, they were widely dispersed. There were also small Jewish communities in the provincial centers near his work. However, he found little in common with them: he said of the Jews of 'Ana, where he was posted at one point, that they were like the local "Arabs" (here meaning "Bedouins" or country people). Their customs, speech and dress were like their Muslim neighbors, and as such unlike Baghdadi Jews, especially the educated strata of the capital. Naji had much more in common socially and intellectually with other government functionaries and professionals posted in the area. These usually had their own club, *Nadi al-Muwadhafin*, where they met to chat, play games, and drink. Naji neither gambled nor drank, but the club was still his main venue of sociability. He also mixed with the local notables, for whom he cared in his professional capacity. He was expected to attend public celebrations and official dinners, together with the *Qa'im maqam*, or district officer. At this level, Naji was integrated into the life of provincial functionaries and detached from his Jewish communal connections and networks, except during periods of leave when he visited his family in Baghdad. At times, in his own words, he forgot that he was a Jew. Once, during an epidemic, Naji encountered difficulty in securing premises for quarantine. The landlord of the designated house tried to renege on the deal at the last minute. To obtain the key, Naji had to be firm and assert his authority, to the extent of slapping the man. This was not unusual conduct in the circumstances, but Naji was later astounded at his own action: "I was a government official," he reflected; "I forgot that I was a Jew!"

Yet he could not forget for long. The political events of the time heightened consciousness of religious divisions, especially with regard to Jews. World War II, combined with events in Palestine, aroused nationalist sentiments colored with Nazi sympathies. The Rashid Ali *coup d'état* in 1941 against the British and their protégés involved attacks on Jews in different parts of Iraq, and Naji was particularly exposed in the western provinces near the Syrian border, especially noted for Arabist sentiments. At one point he had an encounter with Fawzi al-Qawuqchi, the Palestinian militia commander, and his men, there to support Rashid Ali, and withdrawing to Syria at his defeat. Naji had to treat their wounded, and was thanked by Fawzi after initial hesitation to shake the Jew's hand. Later, the creation of the State of Israel heightened anti-Jewish sentiments. While Naji continued to enjoy warm and friendly relations with his patients, local people, notables, and religious dignitaries, he was increasingly targeted by his superiors, medics, and health directors. Some were jealous of his professional success, others resentful of a Jewish presence. As a result he was given the least desirable postings, loaded with extra work, and thus prevented from pursuing more lucrative private practice. He was deterred from resigning by a regulation that doctors retiring from government service could engage in private practice only in the location of their last posting, in this case small provincial centers. He was sacked in 1955, continued to practice in 'Amara, where he became a legend, then moved to Baghdad at the end of the decade.

It is important to tell the story of a Jew precisely because the history of the Jewish presence in the Arab world, as an integral part of these societies and not just as a "pariah" or settler minority, is being forgotten, if not actively erased (by Arab nationalists as well as by Zionists). The Jews are a special case on account of Israel and the conflicts it engendered, and their presence in Iraq and elsewhere in the Arab world was largely ended in the persecutions and mass migrations that followed the formation of the Jewish state. Yet the pressure against the Jews, leading to their migration, is an example of an ongoing quest in the nation-state and of the aim of nationalists: the drive for cultural, social, and religious uniformity, and the intolerance of difference. These drives can be seen from the late Ottoman and post-Ottoman worlds, in the cases of Armenians, Greeks, Assyrians, Alevis, and other smaller groups. Christian communities in the Middle East, ancient and culturally integral to Egypt, Iraq, Syria, and elsewhere, are gradually dwindling, partly due to a constant stream of migration, often under pressure of continuing discrimination. It is estimated that there are now more Iraqi Christians in the USA, Europe, and Australia than in Iraq. The Iraqi state, at its foundation, was obliged to acknowledge difference, especially of the Kurds. Yet, throughout its history it has attempted to reduce or eliminate this recognition. Under the tight repressive Ba'th regime, the quest for Arabization and for the subordination of the Shi'a acquires added dimensions, as an element of insuring total loyalty to the regime and the elimination of any bases for social or cultural autonomy. It feeds directly into communalism: the family, tribe, region, or religious community becomes the unit of security and of connections to the centers of the regime and its party.

The Ba'th regime and the incorporation of civil cociety

What characterizes the Ba'th regime is the authoritarian "étatization" of civil society: destructive repression of political opposition or difference, coupled with an incorporation of all institutions and associations into the state. The Ba'th party itself was de-ideologized in frequent purges, then reduced to a vehicle for loyalty and social control. This was not easy to accomplish: the combination of bloody repression and incorporation proceeded at a gradual pace through the 1970s, particularly with the maneuver of bringing the Communist Party into a common front in government, culminating in the final repression of the party and all its popular associations towards the end of that decade.

The society of citizens was eliminated. They were regimented into the ranks of the party and of loyalty to the ruling clique, their intellectual and cultural products dictated by these considerations. Those that resisted suffered the usual horrors of imprisonment, torture, and execution and often the victimization of their families. The lucky ones escaped to join the ever-expanding communities of exiles (estimated in the millions). Those that remained were reduced to voices of the rulers, often persecuted and humiliated by party and security thugs put in charge of universities and cultural institutions. A recent novel, Hayat Sharara's *idha al-ayamu aghsaqat* (*When Darkness Falls*) (2000) narrates the sorrows, humiliations, and impoverishment of university academics in the 1980s and 1990s. At one point, university teachers, alongside other public employees, are directed to lose weight by a particular date or lose rank and pay, with threat of severance. There followed frantic and painful efforts by rotund middle-aged men to comply. The description of the day of weight registration is tragi-comic, with a large number of professors scrambling to get into a small clinic, exhausted and humiliated. The author, herself a professor of Russian literature, committed suicide soon after she completed the book in 1997. These hardships were exacerbated by the drastic impoverishment of the salaried classes in the years following the Gulf War and the sanctions.

Communalism and the Ba'th regime

Modern nationalism started from a position of rejecting and denouncing communalism (*ta'ifiya*), tribalism, and all sectional interests and loyalties which conflicted with national identity and allegiance. All these communal formations were denounced as backward (*takhaluf*) and corrupt, associated with reactionary forces and religious "superstition." Ba'th ideology, as the very word implies, declared itself a renaissance of the national spirit, forging a unity of purpose and a will to fulfill the eternal mission of the Arab nation. Its slogan: *ummatun 'arabiyatun wahida dhata risalatin khalida* ("one Arab nation with an eternal mission"). In practice, the two Ba'thist regimes of Iraq and Syria, both threw up ruling cliques based on tribal and communal solidarities (see Kienle 1990). The Iraqi Ba'th party and government came to be controlled by allied clans of Tikriti tribes, the Syrian by the Asad family, based on the loyalties of Alawi religious sectarianism. The parties were repeatedly purged to insure complete loyalty and subservience to the ruling cliques. At the same time, the parties became vehicles for the penetration and control of all public institutions and functions, working closely with the multiple security forces. Politics and civil society are totally incorporated into the authoritarian state. Under these conditions, the security and life chances of any individual become dependent on relation to the organs and networks of the regime. For most people, these relations are mediated through connections and solidarities of kinship and community. In the spheres of power, of government, and the military, official rank is subordinated to informal connections of kinship and relations to members of the ruling clique. In the offices of state and public life, it is again connections to the centers of networks of power which procure tenure and promotion.

In the 1990s after the depredations of the second Gulf War, the regime came out openly in support of tribalism. Selected tribal *shaykhs* were officially installed as leaders of their tribes, some of their lands restored (reversing earlier land reforms) and supplied with arms, on condition of loyalty to the regime and ensuring social and political controls in its favor (see Baram 1997: pp. 1–31; and Jabar 2000). By then, of course, they constituted no threat to the regime, but could be useful as instruments of social control. The ideology of this reversal was couched in nationalist rhetoric, extolling tribal solidarity as part of the Arab heritage, and the virtues of old. Of course, "the tribe" at this stage is not a cohesive unit inhabiting its *dira*, or traditional territory: it is dispersed in various parts of the country, many of its members in Baghdad, working in diverse occupations. "Shaykhs" are sometimes urban professionals or businessmen, some with such tenuous connection to their "tribe" that they are satirically labeled "Shaykhs from Taiwan," in parallel with cheap goods imported from that source. They are empowered by the regime to hold tribal "courts" to settle disputes and compensations among their members, with the regime taking a cut of all settlements. The destruction of the civil society of citizens in favour of communalist formations becomes, then, explicit official policy.

Patriarchal and religious themes

One of the few positive elements about the Ba'thist regime was its assault on traditional patriarchal relations and practices. In the 1970s and 1980s, regime policies favored female education and wide participation in the labor market and professional occupations (but not in the echelons of government power). Reforms in family law, started by the Qasim regime, reversed by the Arifs in the 1960s under religious pressure, were then revived by the Ba'thists in the 1970s. These alleviated some of the disadvantages women suffered in family matters under traditional *shari'a* provisions. This may have been done, in part, to challenge and intimidate religious institutions and authorities, and to weaken patriarchal bonds in favor of allegiance to the regime and its ideologies. Many of these positive steps were reversed in the 1990s. "Honor" killing of errant female relatives, for instance, was once again recognized in penal law and given legitimacy by exempting the killers from the penalties for murder. Violence against women was staged dramatically by forces of the regime in the recent campaign against supposed prostitutes: these women were publicly beheaded in Baghdad and other cities. This resort to patriarchal values and practices fitted in with Saddam's increasing resort to religious identification and Islamic rhetoric.

Religious symbols and slogans have come to occupy ever greater space in the regime's rhetoric and practice. During the war against Iran, Saddam countered Iranian Islamic claims by his own, claiming descent from the Prophet and making pious public appearances engaged in prayer and patronage of mosques and shrines. This reversal of the Ba'th's earlier secularist positions was further enhanced after the second Gulf War in the 1990s and Saddam's attempt to jump on the Arab Islamic bandwagon in the hostility to America and the West.

This play on religion had a sectarian dimension of hostility to the Shi'a. The anti-Iranian rhetoric was a thinly disguised attack on what was characterized as a foreign and heretical form of religion. Pan-Arab rhetoric against Iran was explicitly Sunni against its Shi'ism, and the Iraqi Shi'a as such were suspect. The former regime had always combated the institutional autonomy of the Shi'i establishment and persecuted its personnel. At the same time, it strove to procure the compliance of its authorities, by requiring them to issue *fatwas* against its Shi'i enemies. More recently, the newspaper *Babil*, directed by Saddam's son Uday, had waged a sectarian campaign against the Shi'a. They were referred to by the derogatory term of *al-rafidha*, the rejectionists, historically used by their detractors such as the Wahhabis. One article alleged that the mixing of the sexes in some Shi'i religious ceremonies leads to sexual promiscuity, fostered by their *ulama* in order to enhance their numbers! These campaigns were clearly designed to sharpen sectarian solidarities and crystallize Sunni support. It was a further assault on notions and practices of common citizenship and in favor of communalist identities.

Religiosity is not, however, confined to official rhetoric. Observers have reported a marked rise in the signs of popular religiosity. Over the course of the twentieth century, Iraqis may have been sectarian in their allegiances, but were not particularly pious. The Communist Party, for instance, had some of its most prominent sources of support in Shi'ite cities and quarters, and Sunni activists tended more towards pan-Arabism than Islam. Iraq was much less pious than Egypt or even "secular" Turkey. It would seem, however, that the disasters and tragedies that have overtaken the country have fostered a wave of new religious observance of prayer and rituals. It is also reported that there is an upsurge in popular religious practices, such as sufi affiliations and the visitation of tombs. Are these reactions to the insecurity of life and the sense of loss of control over one's fate? Or is it part of the general Islamic wave in the region of piety mixed with a siege mentality of religious nationalism? It is difficult to tell without reliable research. But the religious resurgence can be expected to feed into communalist affiliations and loyalties.

Whither civil society?

What are the prospects for a revival of a civil society of active citizens in Iraq, now that the Saddam regime is ended? What type of new regime would foster or at least permit the regeneration of a public life of politics and culture autonomous from the state? One clear answer is a democratic, pluralist state under the rule of law. But that would seem Utopian under present conditions. The most prominent forces to emerge after the demise of the regime are those of religious institutions, and communal and tribal leaderships. Much as Saddam tried, he could not totally eliminate the autonomy and revenues of the Shi'i institutions and leaderships, and it is these that have come to the fore in the Shi'ite regions to fill the vacuum. Similarly, the Sunni mosques and religious networks, often intermingled with Arab nationalism and loyalty to the defunct regime, have emerged as centers of organization and resistance to the occupying forces in the Sunni areas west of Baghdad. There are no credible independent institutions or associations within the country (though many in exile) which can serve as agents of governance and transformation. A whole generation of Iraqis, the great majority, grew up and reached adulthood under the Ba'th regime, and suffered the terror and depredations of two destructive wars and then the sanctions regime, compounded by regime savagery. The near impossibility of meaningful social research during those years means that we know very little about these generations. General observations indicate that people are increasingly attached to localities and communities in which they find shelter from the continuing insecurities. These are adverse conditions for a civil society of citizens. But we do see, from the example of Iran, that younger generations, once they have a modicum of security and education, are driven by ambition, desire, and the search for fun to challenge the patriarchal and religious authorities ruling over them, in the name of citizenship and liberty. Security, however, is in short supply in Iraq at the time of writing.

Notes

1 For an elaboration of themes of civil society, see Sami Zubaida (2001: pp. 232–49, 2001/2: pp. 20–7).
2 For a modern history of Iraq, see Hanna Batatu (1978); see also Charles Tripp (2002).
3 Material on Jawahiri's biography comes mainly from his own memoirs (1988–91).
4 On the history and institutions of the Shi'a, see Yitzhak Nakash (1994).
5 This is based on interviews with Dr Naji in London in the 1980s. A fuller account can be found in Sami Zubaida (1993: pp. 234–50).

8   Concluding thoughts
Transcending the nation-state?

Haldun Gülalp

A thread running throughout this book has been the tension between the projects of assimilation and multiculturalism. Pursuing assimilation, as in the French concept of citizenship, borrowed with some modifications by Turkey, may result in the suppression or even destruction of distinctive cultures and the imposition of a singular cultural straitjacket on all members of a given nation-state. But asserting the cultural "authenticity" of a people often implies the presence of a unique character that is only transmitted by blood ties and cannot be generalized to others. Combining this assumption with the pursuit of a nation-state results in a concept of citizenship that is exclusive to a particular ethnic or religious group, as was the case in the German, and is still the case in the Israeli, example. Finally, seeking coexistence while retaining the essentialist claims of "authenticity" may result in a divided political entity that not only belies the concept of the *nation*-state but may even degenerate into civil war, as in the case of Lebanon. Clearly, none of these solutions is satisfactory; and, as we saw in the chapters above, this issue mostly remains unresolved.

The problem ultimately seems to originate from the "universalist" assumptions of the modern nation-state. The assumption that there is (or should be) uniformity and homogeneity between equal citizens in the public realm paradoxically generates a system of social inequality, because the imperative to leave particularities behind in order to join the public sphere in effect portends exclusion for those who do not fit the normative ideal defined by the ethnically dominant elite. The assertion of distinct cultural identities and the making of particularistic demands have therefore occasionally culminated in proposals for legal plurality within a single political community (see, for example, Young 1995; Kymlicka 1995; Parekh 2000).

While it is necessary to recognize ethnic, gender, religious, and other such differences in society (collectively described as "cultural diversity") in order to avoid forcing everyone into the single mold defined by powerful elites, the solution should not be the recognition of group rights on a collective basis, because that simply moves the assumption that the individual belongs to a homogeneous collectivity from the national to the subnational level. Defining individuals as members of another imaginary homogeneous community, now below the national level, and endowing that community with rights of autonomy, disempowers those individuals against any possible oppressive practices within the communal hierarchy. Granting communal group rights, that is identifying rights not with reference to individuals but with reference to communities and thereby reinforcing communal identities once they have been (contingently, or even arbitrarily) determined, not only ignores the rights of persons as independent individuals, but may actually contribute to their suppression. In a society of multicultural pluralism, moreover, any number of the distinct cultural groups might be authoritarian. In such a case, the idea of preserving authenticity could readily turn into a license for insular authoritarian cultural practices. Regulating cultural diversity through legal plurality, then, does not engender participatory democracy. It gives priority to the cultural norms of the group over the rights of the individual. Ultimately, it assumes incommensurability between groups of individuals. The claim of preserving cultural specificity cannot be sufficient grounds for granting rights that are specific to a particular social group. The relativistic alternative to universal individual rights may therefore easily degenerate into what has been called "tribalism," where different groups have different sets of rights and are insulated from the larger society in their own particularities (Antonio 2000).

The fundamental reason that a group struggles for particularistic rights is that members of the group have been discriminated against due to membership in that group, which typically has distinct ascriptive attributes and generally experiences a differential social status (Gutmann 2003). If persons are subjected to experiences not originating from their individual achievements but from their group identities, then a possible solution would be to protect the rights of all individuals regardless of their group identity and thereby prevent discrimination. This may necessitate the intervention of the state on behalf of the oppressed or disadvantaged groups. Affirmative action policies that favor historically oppressed groups, such as women or ethnic and racial minorities, are in this sense similar to the intervention of the welfare state on behalf of the dispossessed and the unemployed. Therefore, the issue of relativism inherent in the notion of legal plurality should not be confused with affirmative action policies, which arguably fall within the norms of democracy.

But how to reconcile the notion of affirmative action with the notion of individual rights, since affirmative action necessarily targets a well-defined *group* of people? The answer seems to lie in recognizing the social and historical malleability of these groups. Instead of fixing and freezing identity groups into the political system, diversity could be recognized through individual rights.[1] Individuals would then be free to form alliances and associations based on their changing social needs and/or identities. Any given person combines an indefinite number of socially significant characteristics: ethnicity, gender, race, language, religion, class position, professional status, age, physical ability, sexual orientation, political and philosophical orientation, and so on. This list is actually open-ended because there may be dimensions of identity that are not socially significant or even conceivable now, but may become so in unexpected ways in the future. But even if it were possible to confine them to a manageable number (say, race, religion, and gender), two issues still remain unspecified. One, what is the order of significance between these particular dimensions of identity for the society at large? Two, with which one or several of these dimensions of identity are real individuals going to identify themselves at any point in time? Answering these questions from above, and once and for all, will simply not do. Inscribing such answers into the political system will rule out choices for individuals who may wish to associate with others along one dimension or another, or not at all; and it will also rule out the emergence of new identity formations in accordance with the specificities of a given social structure and its change over time. It will reduce the complexity of every person into a single dimension or a hierarchy of dimensions, which is not necessarily of his or her own choosing.

But if "cultural" diversity were to be granted as individual rights, it would then be up to individuals themselves whether they wish to exercise those rights, which they would now do without fear of exclusion from the larger society or from participation in the political process. They would also determine with whom they wish to associate, depending on their personal priorities with regard to the combination of the socially significant characteristics that they believe they have. These characteristics, moreover, may change over the course of a lifetime. Needs associated with age are a paradigmatic example of the point made here, since age is biological and it inevitably changes over the course of life. It illustrates that a biological factor (which is deemed immutable and thus often informs the politics of race and gender) can nonetheless be a basis of fluid and changing interests. Clearly, the significance of this particular factor, in relation to other socially significant characteristics that one has, will depend on where one is in the lifecycle. One's needs and interests are bound to change with biological age, leading one to identify with different sets of social and political priorities as one moves through life.

With identity rights granted individually, those who freely associate with one another would be able to determine collectively what they feel they need and would negotiate collectively with others in a deliberative process. What is best for them would not be determined from above. Groups would not be fixed and frozen, but would form freely in collaboration with those in similar circumstances and in negotiation with those in different circumstances. A democracy need not ignore the internal diversity of a collectivity; but a political arrangement based on group identity is necessarily intolerant, because it assumes an essential quality that is incommensurable, non-negotiable, and exclusive. Although, as opposition movements, identity politics may be, and indeed have been, useful in identifying the structural conditions that at any point in time create systematic inequalities between groups in society, they are not a democratic basis on which a project for power could be built. It is easy to see that if an identity movement successfully gains power, such as in a religious fundamentalist regime, then the outcome is bound to be exclusionary and non-democratic.

But how does the question of diversity within a national community affect the practice of democracy, which currently takes the nation-state as its framework? Modern democracy has two distinct, and potentially contradictory, historical origins. One is the Athenian model of "active citizens," where the collectivity rather than the individual has primacy and, therefore, participation in the collective decision-making process (for those who have the required status) is more an obligation than a right. The other is the Enlightenment model of the "right-bearing citizens," where the individual has inviolable rights, including the right not to participate in the political process, and the individual has primacy over the collectivity (Manville 1990; Dunn 1992; Ignatieff 1995; Pocock 1995; Wood 1995). The tension between these two principles of democracy translates into the following dilemma. On the one hand, democracy as a political regime presupposes the free will of the independent individual and, as such, formally recognizes him or her as a citizen endowed with rights. The individual is assumed to be rational, self-interested, and independent in thought and judgment; hence, as such, individuals interact with each other as free and equal citizens. On the other hand, democracy also presupposes a community that shares a common public space. A community, by definition, has limits. It necessarily implies a well-defined (however imaginary) set of common characteristics and is always exclusionary. A community also implies the imperative (or the contingency) of living together. Without this necessity of living together, the question of democracy, as a system of self-rule by the political collectivity, would not have arisen. Without having to share a common set of problems, the project of finding collective solutions and making collective decisions would not have been an issue. Thus, even though the democratic individual is assumed to be independent, democracy is only possible within a community that already exists. The "independent" individual is actually a member of a given "community."

This abstract dilemma can be observed at the concrete level in the framework of the nation-state, which has been the site of liberal democracy in the modern period. On the one hand, the nation-state defines the strict boundaries of the community of citizens. As such, citizenship in the nation-state implies an exclusive membership in a community, hence a national identity. On the other hand, the nation-state (ideally) follows universal rules in its treatment of citizens. As such, citizenship implies equality before the law and the possession of a set of rights vis-à-vis the state and other citizens. In democratic nation-states, the latter includes the right to participate in political decision-making. Thus, citizenship has the dual meaning of identity, which is exclusive, and participation, which is inclusive. Within the nation-state framework, citizenship rights of participation are necessarily limited to a well-defined community of people.

This situation raises a question with regard to one of the fundamental assumptions of democracy. If, as suggested above, democracy presupposes the existence of a community with a shared identity, does the creation of a multiplicity of cultural communities with distinct identities within a single nation-state shake the foundations of democracy? Do not, then, the concept of the "nation" and the identity claims of the nation-state need a revision? Is it not necessary to redefine the democratic community on a basis other than the "primordial" identity? Is it not, in other words, necessary to separate "nationality" from "citizenship" in order to maintain democracy?

We have already argued that, considering the tension between the universalist aspirations and the essentialist assumptions of the nation-state, the democratic principles of citizenship are best advanced in a model of state that is no longer formally identified with a particular national identity. In the age of globalization, moreover, not only are nationality and citizenship separated due to the rise of multicultural societies, but territory and governance are also separated due to the creation of supranational institutions that limit nation-state sovereignty. The weakening of the command of nation-states over their citizens may have led some of them to change both their legal–formal and ideological definitions of citizenship in favor of recognizing cultural diversity; but globalization also engenders questions about democratic participation, which can no longer be resolved at the level of the nation-state. The nation-state model is unable to meet the needs of a global order. It cannot contain the structures of sovereignty in a global system where national borders become less and less relevant to people's lives, or may even become hindrances rather than facilitators to the pursuit of the collective social good.

Our received notions of citizenship and democracy remain confined to the framework of the territorially circumscribed nation-state. The nation-state still appears as the pertinent political unit for the exercise of democracy, but globalization has been weakening the sovereignty of the nation-state on a number of levels. Today, although the formal framework of the sovereign nation-state remains, the substance of sovereignty is often shared among multiple actors at the global, regional, and local levels. By challenging the nation-state, globalization has also been challenging the received framework of democracy (Connolly 1991; von Bredow 1998; Holden 2000). While this shrinkage of absolute territorial sovereignty may be a good thing for the citizens of an oppressive nation-state, for instance if they can successfully appeal to extra-national sources of authority for the protection of their human rights, its broader implications for democracy in general are more ambiguous. Democracy, in its received form, presupposes a sovereign state and a community to which the state is responsible. In a system of multiple sources and layers of authority, who will be held responsible for the well-being of the citizens of a nation-state? What institutions beyond the nation-state will become responsible for safeguarding "citizenship" rights? Clearly, a system of supranational citizenship would require the creation of a unified set of supranational political institutions that regulate the affairs of citizens, including first of all the formal identification and recognition of their citizenship status, with all the attendant rights, as well as the protection and enforcement of those rights.

Conversely, in a system of transnational institutions that share state sovereignty, who exactly makes up the community to which these institutions may be held accountable? We had noted earlier that democratic participation requires a well-defined community, while a community implies membership and, hence, exclusion. How, then, are we to define the democratic community beyond the nation? How and by what criteria are we to measure the commonality between the members of that community? The answer in this case seems to be somewhat easier, even if currently unattainable: a supranational democracy requires at least a common inclination toward, and a common language of, negotiation and participation. Community in such a political association would be formed, not along the lines of imaginary (and divisive) national identities, but around the universal principles of equality, freedom, and political participation.

Notes

1 Incidentally, this is how the "Framework Convention for the Protection of National Minorities" (1995) of the Council of Europe addresses the issue. It frames the rights of minorities as the "further realization of human rights and fundamental freedoms," and states in Article 3 that "(1) Every person belonging to a national minority shall have the right freely to choose to be treated or not to be treated as such and no disadvantage shall result from this choice or from the exercise of the rights which are connected to that choice" and "(2) Persons belonging to national minorities may exercise the rights and enjoy the freedoms flowing from the principles enshrined in the present framework Convention individually as well as in community with others."

References

Archives

Turkish Republic, Prime Ministry's Republican Archive – *Basbakanlik Cumhuriyet Arsivi* (BCA)
Great Britain, Foreign Office: Political Departments, General Correspondence from 1906 (FO)
Records of the Department of State Relating to Internal Affairs of Turkey 1930–44 (SD)

Turkish Grand National Assembly

Düstur
TBMM Zabit Ceridesi

Newspapers

An-Nahar
As-Safir
Eleutherotypia
Ethnos
Kathimerini
Ta Nea
To Vima
The Daily Star
The Hellenic Star
The New York Times
The Observer

Statistical yearbooks

Turkish Republic, Prime Ministry – *Istatistik Yilligi*:
vol. 2, 1929
vol. 7, 1934–5
vol. 10, 1938–9.

Books and articles

Abramov, Z. (1976) *Perpetual Dilemma: Jewish Religion in the Jewish State*. Rutherford, NJ: Fairleigh Dickinson University Press.

Ahmad, F. (1969) *The Young Turks: The CUP in Turkish Politics, 1908–1914*. Oxford: Oxford University Press.

Ahmad, F. (1993) *The Making of Modern Turkey*. London: Routledge.

Aktar, A. (2000) *Varlik Vergisi ve 'Türklestirme' Politikalan* [The Wealth Tax and 'Turkification' Policies]. Istanbul: Iletisim, 2000.

al-Hajj, K. (1961) *Al-Ta'ifah al-Banna'ah, aw falsafat al-Mithaq al-Watani* [Philosophy of the National Pact]. Beirut.

al-Jawahiri, M. M. (1988–91) *Dhikrayati*, 2 volumes. Damascus: Dar al-Rafidain.

al-Khazen, F. (1991) *The Communal Pact of National Identities*. Oxford: Center for Lebanese Studies.

Alaettin, I. (ed.) (1930) *Yeni Türk Lugati* [New Turkish Dictionary]. Istanbul: Kanaat.

Alivizatos, N. (1999) "A new role for the Greek Church?", *Journal of Modern Greek Studies*, 17.

Anagnostou, D. (2001) "Breaking the cycle of nationalism: the EU, regional policy and the minority of Western Thrace, Greece," *South European Society and Politics*, 6(1), Summer 2001.

Antonio, R. J. (2000) "After postmodernism: reactionary tribalism," *American Journal of Sociology,* 106(2).

Archibugi, D. and D. Held (eds) (1995) *Cosmopolitan Democracy: An Agenda for a New World Order*. Cambridge: Polity Press.

Atatürk'ün Söylev ve Demeçleri, I–III (1997) [Ataturk's Speeches and Declarations, I–III]. Ankara: Atatürk Arastirma Merkezi.

Bade, K. J. (ed.) (1984) *Bevölkerung, Arbeitsmarkt und Wanderung in Deutsch(land) seit der Mitte des 19.Jh.s*, vol. 1. Ostfilden, Scripta Mercaturae Verlag.

Bade, K. J. (1994) "Politik in der Einwanderungssituation: Migration – Integration – Minderheiten" in idem (ed.) *Deutsche im Ausland – Fremde in Deutschland – Migration in Geschichte und Gegenwart*. München: Verlag C.H. Beck.

Bali, R. N. (1999) *Cumhuriyet Yillarinda Türkiye Yahudileri: Bir Türklestirme Serüveni (1923–1945)* [Turkish Jews under the Turkish Republic: An Episode of Turkification (1923–1945)]. Istanbul: Iletisim.

Bali, R. N. (2001) *Musa'nin Evlatlari Cumhuriyet'in Yurttaslari* [The Children of Moses, the Citizens of the Republic]. Istanbul: Iletisim.

Balibar, E. (2004) "Dissonances within *Laicite*," *Constellations*, 11(3).

Banac, I. and K. Verdery (eds) (1995) *National Character and National Ideology in inter-war Eastern Europe*. New Haven: Yale Center for International and Area Studies.

Baram, A. (1997) "Neo-tribalism in Iraq: Saddam Hussein's tribal policies 1991–96," *International Journal of Middle East Studies*, 29(1).

Barry, B. (2001) *Culture and Equality*. Cambridge, MA: Harvard University Press.

Batatu, H. (1978) *The Old Social Classes and the Revolutionary Movements of Iraq: A Study of Iraq's Old Landed and Commercial Classes, and of its Communists, Ba'thists and Free Officers*. Princeton, NJ: Princeton University Press.

Bayrak, M. (1993) *Kürtler ve Ulusal-Demokratik Mücadeleleri* [The Kurds and their National-Democratic Struggles]. Ankara: Üzge Yayinlari.

Behar, C. (ed.) (1996) *The Population of the Ottoman Empire and Turkey*, Historical Statistics Series, vol. 2. Ankara: State Institute of Statistics.

Benhabib, S. (ed.) (1996) *Democracy and Difference: Contesting the Boundaries of the Political*. Princeton, NJ: Princeton University Press.

Benhabib, S. (2002) *The Claims of Culture: Equality and Diversity in the Global Era*. Princeton, NJ: Princeton University Press.

Berman, S. (1997) "Civil Society and Political Institutionalization," *American Behavioral Scientist*, 40(5), March/April.

Besikçi, I. (1977) *Kürtlerin 'Mecburi Iskan'i* [The 'Forced Resettlement' of the Kurds]. Istanbul: Komal.

Birinci Türk Tarih Kongresi (1933) [First Turkish History Congress]. Ankara: T.C. Maarif Vekaleti.

Bohman, J. and M. Lutz-Bachman (eds) (1997) *Perpetual Peace: Essays on Kant's Cosmopolitan Ideal*. Cambridge, MA: MIT Press.

Breuilly, J. (1982) *Nationalism and the State*. New York: St Martin's Press.

Brubaker, R. (1992) *Citizenship and Nationhood in France and Germany*. Cambridge, MA: Harvard University Press.

Cagaptay, S. (2003a) "Crafting the Turkish nation: Kemalism and Turkish nationalism in the 1930s," Yale University, Ph.D. dissertation, May.

Cagaptay, S. (2003b) "European Union reforms diminish the role of the Turkish military: Ankara knocking on Brussels' door," *Policywatch*, no. 781, The Washington Institute for Near East Policy, 12 August at http://www.washingtoninstitute.org/watch/index.htm.

Cagaptay, S. (2003c) "Citizenship and nationalism in inter-war Turkey," *Nations and Nationalism*, 9(4), October.

Carens, J. H. (1998) "Why Naturalization Should be Easy" in N. M. J. Pickus (ed.) *Immigration and Citizenship in the 21st Century*. Lanham, MD: Rowman and Littlefield.

Carr, E. H. (1945) *Nationalism and After*. London: Macmillan.

Cohn-Bendit, D. and T. Schmid (1992) *Heimat Babylon. Das Wagnis der multikulturellen Demokratie*. Hamburg: Hoffmann and Campe.

Connolly, W. E. (1991) "Democracy and territoriality," *Millennium: Journal of International Studies*, 20(3).

Cumhuriyet Halk Firkasi Nizamnamesi (1927) [By-Laws of the Republican People's Party]. Ankara.

Dahrendorf, R. (1988) *The Modern Social Conflict: An Essay on the Politics of Liberty*. Berkeley, CA: University of California Press.

Davis, U. (1997) *Citizenship and the State: A Comparative Study of Citizenship Legislation in Israel, Jordan, Palestine, Syria and Lebanon*. Reading: Garnett Publishing.

De Witte, B. (2001) "Politics vs. Law in the EU's approach to ethnic minorities," European University Institute, Working Papers, RSC no. 2000/4, Florence.

Deringil, S. (1998) *The Well-Protected Domains: Ideology and Legitimation of Power in the Ottoman Empire, 1876–1909*. London: I.B.Tauris.

Diamond, J. (1986) *Homeland or Holyland? The Canaanite Critique of Israel*. Bloomington, IN: Indiana University Press.

Dieckhoff, A. (2000) *La nation dans tous ses états. Les identités nationales en mouvement*. Paris: Flammarion.

Dieckhoff, A. (1993) "La maturation politique d'une minorité ethnique," *Revue du monde musulman et de la Méditerranée*, 68/69.

Dieckhoff, A. (1999) "Israel: the Pluralization of a National Identity" in H. Kriesi *et al.* (eds) *Nation and National Identity: The European Experience in Perspective*. Zurich: Rüegger.

Dieckhoff, A. (1993) *L'invention d'une nation. Israel et la modernité politique*. Paris: Gallimard. (English-language edition: *The Invention of a Nation: Zionist Thought and the Making of Modern Israel*. London: Hurst and New York: Columbia University Press, 2003).

Dietz, B. (1999) "Jugendliche Aussiedler in Deutschland: Risiken und Chancen der Integration" in K. J. Bade and J. Oltmer (eds) *Aussiedler: Deutsche Einwanderer aus Osteuropa*, IMIS-Schriften 8. Osnabrück: Universitätsverlag Rasch.

Dimitropoulos, P. (2001) *Government and Church: a difficult relationship*. Athens: Kritiki.

Dumont, L. (1991) *L'idéologie allemande. France–Allemagne et retour*. Paris: Gallimard.

Dündar, F. (2001) *Ittihat ve Terakki'nin Müslümanlari Iskan Politikasi* [CUP's resettlement policy of the Muslims]. Istanbul: Iletisim.

Dunn, J. (ed.) (1992) *Democracy: The Unfinished Journey*. New York: Oxford University Press.

Ersanli, B. (2003) *Iktidar ve Tarih* [Power and History]. Istanbul: Iletisim.

Faist, T. (2004) "Dual Citizenship as Overlapping Membership" in D. Joly (ed.) *International Migration in the New Millennium. Global Movement and Settlement*. Aldershot, UK: Ashgate.

Falk, R. and A. Strauss (2001) "Toward global parliament," *Foreign Affairs*, Jan/Feb.

Frazee, C. (1979) "The Orthodox Church of Greece in the last Fifteen Years" in J. T. Koumoulides (ed.) *Greece: Past and Present*. Indiana: Ball State University.

Gellner, E. (1983) *Nations and Nationalism*. Oxford: Basil Blackwell.

Georgiadou, V. (1995) "Greek Orthodoxy and the politics of nationalism," *International Journal of Politics, Culture and Society*, 9(2).

Giddens, A. (1995) *The Nation-State and Violence*. Cambridge: Polity Press.

Gökalp, Z. (1952) *Türkçülügün Esaslari* [The Principles of Turkism]. Istanbul: Türk Tarih Kurumu.

Gosewinkel, D. (1998) "Citizenship and Nationhood: The Historical Development of the German Case" in U. K. Preuss and F. Requejo (eds) *European Citizenship, Multiculturalism and the State*. Baden-Baden: Nomos Verl.-Ges.

Grossman, D. (1993) *Sleeping on a Wire: Conversations with Palestinians in Israel*. London: Jonathan Cape.

Gülalp, H. (2003) *Kimlikler Siyaseti: Türkiye'de Siyasal Islamin Temelleri* [Politics of Identities: Foundations of Political Islam in Turkey]. Istanbul: Metis.

Gülalp, H. (2005) "The Turkish Route to Democracy: Domestic Reform via Foreign Policy" in S. Wells and L. Künhardt (eds) *The Crisis in Transatlantic Relations*, ZEI Discussion Paper, C143. Bonn: Center for European Integration Studies.

Gutmann, A. (ed.) (1994) *Multiculturalism: Examining the Politics of Recognition*. Princeton, NJ: Princeton University Press.

Gutmann, A. (2003) *Identity in Democracy*. Princeton, NJ: Princeton University Press.

Hanf, T. (1993) *Coexistence in Wartime Lebanon: Decline of a State and Rise of a Nation*. London: I.B. Tauris.

Held, D. (1991) "Democracy, the Nation-State and the Global System" in idem (ed.) *Political Theory Today*. Stanford: Stanford University Press.

Held, D. (2000) "The Changing Contours of Political Community: Rethinking Democracy in the Context of Globalization" in B. Holden (ed.) *Global Democracy: Key Debates*. London: Routledge.

Helman, S. (1997) "Militarism and the Construction of Community," *Journal of Political and Military Sociology*, 25(2), Winter.

Herzfeld, M. (1986) *Ours Once More: Folklore, Ideology, and the Making of Modern Greece*. New York: Pella.

Herzfeld, M. (1997) *Cultural Intimacy: Social Poetics in the Nation-State*. London: Routledge.

Herzfeld, M. (2002) "The European Self: Rethinking an Attitude" in A. Pagden (ed.) *The Idea of Europe: From Antiquity to the European Union*. Washington, DC: Woodrow Wilson Center Press, and Cambridge: Cambridge University Press.

Hirschon, R. (ed.) (2003) *Crossing the Aegean: An Appraisal of the 1923 Compulsory Population Exchange Between Greece and Turkey*. Oxford: Berghahn Books.

Hobsbawm, E. J. (1977) *The Age of Revolution*. London: Abacus.

Hobsbawm, E. J. (1992) *Nations and Nationalism Since 1780: Programme, Myth, Reality*. Cambridge: Cambridge University Press.

Holden, B. (ed.) (2000) *Global Democracy: Key Debates*. London: Routledge.

Ignatieff, M. (1995) "The Myth of Citizenship" in R. Beiner (ed.) *Theorizing Citizenship*. Albany: SUNY Press.

Ignatieff, M. (2001) *Human Rights as Politics and Idolatry*. Princeton, NJ: Princeton University Press.

Inan, A. (1969) *Medeni Bilgiler ve Atatürk'ün El Yazilari* [Civics and Atatürk's Manuscripts]. Ankara: Türk Tarih Kurumu.

Jabar, F. (2000) "Shaykhs and ideologues: detribalization and retribalization in Iraq," *Middle East Report*, no. 215, Summer.

Jiryis, S. (1968) *The Arabs in Israel.* Beirut: Institute for Palestine Studies.
Karal, E. Z. (1981) "The Principles of Kemalism" in A. Kazancigil and E. Özbudun (eds) *Atatürk: Founder of a Modern State.* London: C. Hurst and Co.
Karpat, K. (1973) *An Inquiry into the Social Foundations of Nationalism in the Ottoman State.* Princeton University, Center of International Studies, Research Monograph, no. 39.
Karpat, K. (1982) "Millets and Nationality: The Roots of Incongruity of Nation and State in the Post-Ottoman Era" in B. Braude and B. Lewis (eds) *Christians and Jews in the Ottoman Empire,* vol. 1. New York: Holmes and Meier.
Karpat, K. (1991) "The Republican People's Party" in M. Heper and J. Landau (eds) *Political Parties and Democracy in Turkey.* London: I.B. Tauris.
Kastoryano, R. (1997) "Participation transnationale et citoyenneté: Les immigrés en Europe," *Culture et Conflits,* no. 28, Winter.
Kastoryano, R. (1997) *La France, l'Allemagne et leurs immigrés. Négocier l'identité.* Paris: Armand Colin. (English language edition: *Negotiating Identities, States and Immigrants in France and Germany.* Princeton, NJ: Princeton University Press, 2002.)
Katzenstein, P. (1987) *Policy and Politics in West Germany: The Growth of a Semi-Sovereign State.* Philadelphia, PA: Temple University Press.
Katzenstein, P. (ed.) (1997) *Tamed Power: Germany in Europe.* Ithaca, NY: Cornell University Press.
Kazgan, G. (1983) "Milli Türk Devletinin Kurulusu ve Göçler" [The Establishment of the Turkish Nation-State and Migrations], *Cumhuriyet Dönemi Türkiye Ansiklopedisi.* Istanbul: Iletisim.
Kent, G. D. (1971) *The political influence of the Orthodox Church of Greece,* Ph.D. thesis, Political Science, University of Colorado.
Keyder, Ç. (1987) *State and Class in Turkey: A Study in Capitalist Development.* London: Verso.
Keyder, Ç. (1997) "The Ottoman Empire" in M. von Hagen and K. Barkey (eds) *After Empire.* Boulder, CO: Westview Press.
Khairallah, D. L. (1994) "Secular Democracy: A Viable Alternative to the Confessional System" in D. Collings (ed.) *Peace for Lebanon? From War to Reconstruction.* Boulder, CO: Lynne Rienner.
Kienle, E. (1990) *Ba'th vs. Ba'th: The Conflict Between Syria and Iraq 1968–89.* London: I.B. Tauris.
King, R. (1986) *The State in Modern Society.* London: Macmillan.
Klein, C. (1977) *Le caractère juif de l'Etat d'Israël.* Paris: Cujas.
Kojaman, Y. (2001) *The Maqam Music Tradition of Iraq.* Published by the author: London.
Kökdemir, N. (ed.) (1952) *Eski ve Yeni Toprak Iskan Hükümleri Uygulamasi Kilavuzu* [Guide to the Application of Old and New Land and Resettlement Decisions]. Ankara.
Kokosalakis, N. (1987) "Religion and Modernization in 19th century Greece," *Social Compass,* 34(2/3).

Kokosalakis, N. (1995) "Church and State in the Orthodox Context with Special Reference to Greece" in P. Antes, P. DeMarco and A. Nesti (eds) *Identita Europea e diversita religiosa nel mutamento contemporaeo.* Florence: Angelo Pontecorboli Editore.

Konidaris, I. (2003) "The legal parameters of Church and State relations in Greece" in T. Couloumbis, T. Kariotis and F. Bellou (eds) *Greece in the Twentieth Century.* London: Frank Cass.

Kretzmer, D. (1990) *The Legal Status of the Arabs in Israel.* Boulder, CO: Westview.

Kushner, D. (1977) *The Rise of Turkish Nationalism.* London: Frank Cass.

Kymlicka, W. (1995) *Multicultural Citizenship: A Liberal Theory of Minority Rights.* Oxford: Clarendon Press.

Leca, J. (1986) "Individualisme et citoyenneté" in P. Birnbaum and J. Leca (eds) *Sur l'individualisme.* Paris: Presses of the FNSP.

Leca, J. (1992) "Nationalité et citoyenneté dans l'Europe des immigrations" in J. Costa-Lascoux and P. Weil (eds) *Logiques d'état et immigration en Europe.* Paris: Kimé.

Lehmbruch, G. (1967) *Proporzdemokratie: Politisches System und politische Kultur in der Schweiz und in Österreich.* Tübingen.

Lijphart, A. (1977) *Democracy in Plural Societies. A Comparative Exploration.* New Haven, NY: Yale University Press.

Linklater, A. (1998) "Cosmopolitan Citizenship," *Citizenship Studies*, 2(1).

Lustick, I. (1980) *Arabs in the Jewish State: Israel's Control of a National Minority.* Austin and London: University Press of Texas.

McCarthy, J. (1982) *The Arab World, Turkey and the Balkans (1878–1914): A Handbook of Historical Statistics.* Boston, MA: G. K. Hall.

McCarthy, J. (1995) *Death and Exile: The Ethnic Cleansing of the Ottoman Muslims, 1821–1922.* Princeton, NJ: Darwin Press.

Makdisi, U. (2000) *The Culture of Sectarianism: Community, History, and Violence in Nineteenth-Century Ottoman Lebanon.* Berkeley, CA: University of California Press.

Makrides, V. (1991) "Orthodoxy as a Conditio sine qua non: Religion and State/Politics in Modern Greece from a Socio-historical Perspective," *Ostkirchliche Studien*, 40.

Manitakis, A. (2000) "H Autokefali Ecclesia tis Ellados metaksi Kratous kai Ethnous" [The Autocephalous Church of Greece between State and Nation]. *Domes kai sxeseis eksousias sti simerini Ellada.*

Manville, P. B. (1990) *The Origins of Citizenship in Ancient Athens.* Princeton, NJ: Princeton University Press.

Marshall, T. H. (1964) *Class, Citizenship and Social Development.* New York: Doubleday and Company.

Ménassa, B. (ed.) (1995) Constitution Libanaise. *Text et commentaires et Accord de Taëf.*

Messarra, A. (1986) "Les chances de survie du système consociatif libanais. D'une consociation sauvage […] à un modèle consociatif rationalisé" in T. Hanf *et al.* (eds) *La Société de Concordance.* Beirut.

Messarra, A. (1994) *Théorie générale du système politique libanais. Essai comparé sur les fondements et les perspectives d'évolution d'un système consensuel de gouvernement.* Paris.

Messarra, A. (1997) *Le pacte libanais. Le message d'universalité et ses contraintes.* Beirut.

Morris, B. (1987) *The Birth of the Palestinian Refugee Problem, 1947–1949.* Cambridge: Cambridge University Press.

Münz, R. and R. Ulrich (1998) "Germany and its immigrants: a socio-demographic analysis," *Journal of Ethnic and Migration Studies,* 24(1), January.

Münz, R., W. Seifer and R. Ulrich (1997) *Zuwanderung nach Deutschland: Strukturen, Wirkungen, Perspektiven.* Frankfurt: Campus Verlag.

Nakash, Y. (1994) *The Shi'is of Iraq.* Princeton, NJ: Princeton University Press.

Papadopoulou, L. (2000) "On the Issue of the identity cards," *The Constitution* [*To Syntagma*], 4/5, Jul/Oct.

Papastathis, C. (1995) "State and Church in Greece" in G. Robbers (ed.) *State and Church in the European Union.* Baden-Baden: Nomos Verlagsgesellschaft.

Parekh, B. (2000) *Rethinking Multiculturalism.* Cambridge, MA: Harvard University Press.

Passerini, L. (2002) "From the Ironies of Identity to the Identities of Irony" in A. Pagden (ed.) *The Idea of Europe: From Antiquity to the European Union.* Washington, DC: Woodrow Wilson Center Press, and Cambridge: Cambridge University Press.

Peker, R. (1931) *CHF Programinin Izahi* [Explanation of the Program of the Republican People's Party]. Ankara: Ulus Matbaasi.

Perthes, V. (1994) *Der Libanon nach dem Bürgerkrieg. Von Ta'if zum gesellschaftlichen Konsens?* Baden-Baden.

Phillips, A. (1995) *The Politics of Presence.* Oxford: Clarendon Press.

Phillips, A. (1999) *Which Equalities Matter?* Cambridge: Polity Press.

Picard, E. (1996) *Lebanon: A Shattered Country.* New York and London: Holmes and Meier.

Pickus, N. M. J. (1998) "Introduction" in idem (ed.) *Immigration and Citizenship in the 21st Century.* Lanham, MD: Rowman and Littlefield.

Pittard, E. (1924) *Les Races et l'histoire: Introduction ethnologique à l'histoire.* Paris: La Renaissance du Livre.

Pocock, J. G. A. (1995) "The Ideal of Citizenship Since Classical Times" in R. Beiner (ed.) *Theorizing Citizenship.* Albany, NY: SUNY Press.

Poggi, G. (1978) *The Development of the Modern State: A Sociological Introduction.* Stanford, CA: Stanford University Press.

Poggi, G. (1990) *The State: Its Nature, Development, and Prospects.* Cambridge: Polity Press.

Rabbath, E. (1973) *La formation historique du Liban politique et constitutionnel: Essai de synthèse.* Beirut.

Reinkowski, M. (1995) *Filastin, Filistin und Eretz Israel: die späte osmanische Herrschaft über Palästina in der arabischen, türkischen und israelischen Historiographie.* Berlin: K. Schwarz.

Rexine, J. (1972) "The Church in contemporary Greek society," *Diakonia*, 7.

Risse, T. and D. Engelmann-Martin (2002) "Identity Politics and European Integration: The Case of Germany" in A. Pagden (ed.) *The Idea of Europe: From Antiquity to the European Union*. Washington, DC: Woodrow Wilson Center Press, and Cambridge: Cambridge University Press.

Rothschild, J. (ed.) (1998) *East Central Europe Between the Two World Wars, A History of East Central Europe*, vol. 9. Seattle, WA: University of Washington Press.

Roudometof, V. (2001) *Nationalism, Globalization, and Orthodoxy: The Social Origins of Ethnic Conflict in the Balkans*. Connecticut: Greenwood Press.

Saadeh, S. (2000) *Antun Saadeh and Democracy in Geographic Syria*. London: Folios.

Saadeh, S. (1993) *The Social Structure of Lebanon: Democracy or Servitude?* Beirut: Editions Dar An-Nahar.

Saadeh, S. (1999) "Qawanin al-Raqabah fi Lubnan ma Ba'd al-Harb" [Censorship Laws in Postwar Lebanon] in W. Mubarak (ed.) *Bina' al-Muwatiniyyah fi Lubnan* [Building Citizenship in Lebanon]. Beirut: Lebanese American University.

Saadeh, S. (2002) "Basic Issues Concerning Personal Status Laws in Lebanon" in T. Scheffler (ed.) *Religion: Between Violence and Reconciliation*. Beirut: DMG.

Salam, N. (1994) "Individu et citoyen au Liban" in F. Kiwan (ed.) *Le Liban aujourd'hui*. Paris.

Salamé, G. (1994) "Small is Pluralistic: Democracy as an Instrument of Civil Peace" in G. Salamé (ed.) *Democracy Without Democrats? The Renewal of Politics in the Muslim World*. London: I.B. Tauris.

Scheffler, T. (2002) "Introduction: Religion Between Violence and Reconciliation" in idem (ed.) *Religion Between Violence and Reconciliation*. Beirut: DMG.

Schmidt, P. and S. Weick (1999) "Intégration sociale des étrangers en Allemagne," *Revue de l'OFCE*, no. 69, April.

Schuck, P. H. (1998) "Plural Citizenships" in N. M. J. Pickus (ed.) *Immigration and Citizenship in the 21st Century*. Lanham, MD: Rowman and Littlefield.

Segev, T. (1993) *The Seventh Million: The Israelis and the Holocaust*. New York: Henry Holt.

Sen, F. and Y. Karakasoglu (1994) *F. Almanya'da yasiyan Türklerin ve diger yabancilarin seçme ve seçilme hakki, partiler ve çifte vatandaslik üzerine görüsleri*. Zentrum für Türkeistudien, Essen, September.

Sharara, H. (2000) *Idha al-Ayamu Aghsaqat*. Beirut: Al-Mu'assasa al-Arabiya lil-Dirasat wal-Nashr.

Sherrard, P. (1959) *The Greek East and the Latin West: A Study in the Christian Tradition*. New York: Oxford University Press.

Slaughter, A-M. (2003) "Everyday global governance," *Daedalus*, **132**(1).

Smooha, S. (1990) "Minority status in an ethnic democracy: the status of the Arab minority in Israel," *Ethnic and Racial Studies*, 13(3).

Smooha, S. (1997) "Ethnic democracy: Israel as an archetype," *Israel Studies*, 2(2), Fall.

Soysal, I. (1983) *Türkiye'nin Siyasi Antlasmalari* [Political Treaties of Turkey]. Ankara: Türk Tarih Kurumu.

Soysal, Y. N. (1994) *Limits of Citizenship: Migrants and Postnational Membership in Europe*. Chicago, IL: University of Chicago.

Spiro, P. J. (1999) *Embracing Dual Nationality*. International Migration Policy Program, Carnegie Endowment for International Peace; Occasional Paper, no. 1.

Tachau, F. (1972) "The search for national identity among the Turks," *Die Welt des Islams*, New Series, 8(2/3).

Taylor, C. (1992) "Les institutions dans la vie nationale" in *Rapprocher les solitudes: Ecrits sur le fédéralisme et le nationalisme au Canada* (texts recollected by G. Laforest). Saint-Foy: Presses de l'Université de Laval.

Tekeli, I. (1990) "Osmanli Imparatorlugu'ndan Günümüze Nüfusun Zorunlu Yer Degistirmesi," *Toplum ve Bilim*, no. 50.

Torpey, J. (2001) "The Great War and the Birth of the Modern Passport System" in J. Caplan and J. Torpey (eds) *Documenting Individual Identity: The Development of State Practices in the Modern World*. Princeton, NJ: Princeton University Press.

Tripp, C. (2002) *A History of Iraq*. Cambridge: Cambridge University Press.

Türk Tarihinin Ana Hatlarina Methal (1930). Istanbul: Devlet Matbaasi.

Turner, B. S. (ed.) (1993) *Citizenship and Social Theory*. London: Sage.

Van der Veer, P. and H. Lehmann (eds) (1999) *Nation and Religion: Perspectives on Europe and Asia*. Princeton, NJ: Princeton University Press.

Vandenberg, A. (ed.) (2000) *Citizenship and Democracy in a Global Era*. New York: St Martin's Press.

Von Bredow, W. (1998) "The Changing Character of National Borders," *Citizenship Studies*, 2(3).

Walzer, M. (1994) "The Civil Society Argument" in C. Mouffe (ed.) *Radical Democracy*. London: Verso.

Weil, P. and R. Hansen (eds) (1999) *Nationalité et citoyenneté en Europe*. Paris: La Découverte.

Wilmsen, E. N. and P. McAllister (eds) (1996) *The Politics of Difference: Ethnic Premises in a World of Power*. Chicago, IL: University of Chicago Press.

Wood, E. M. (1995) "The Demos versus 'We the People': From Ancient to Modern Conceptions of Citizenship" in idem (ed.) *Democracy Against Capitalism*. Cambridge: Cambridge University Press.

Yalçin-Heckmann, L. (1995) "The perils of ethnic associational life in Europe: Turkish migrants in Germany and in France," paper submitted to the workshop on "Culture, Communication and Discourse: Negotiating Difference in Multi-Ethnic Alliances" organized by ICCCR, Universities of Manchester and Keele, 9–12 December.

Yegen, M. (2004) "Citizenship and Ethnicity in Turkey," *Middle Eastern Studies*, 40(6), November.

Yiannaras, C. (1976) *Chapters of Political Theology*. Athens: Papazisi.

Young, I. M. (1995) "Polity and Group Difference: A Critique of the Ideal of Universal Citizenship" in R. Beiner (ed.) *Theorizing Citizenship*. Albany: SUNY Press.

Zentrum für Türkeistudien (1992) *Konsumgewohnheiten und wirtschaftliche Situation der türkischen Bevölkerung in der Bundesrepublik Deutschland*. Essen, September.

Zentrum für Türkeistudien (1993) *The Economic and Political Impact of Turkish Migration in Germany*. Essen, March.

Zubaida, S. (1991) "Community, Class and Minorities in Iraqi Politics" in R. Fernea and R. Louis (eds) *The Iraqi Revolution of 1958: the Old Social Classes Revisited*. London: I.B. Tauris.

Zubaida, S. (1993) "Naji: An Iraqi Country Doctor" in E. Burke III (ed.) *Struggle and Survival in the Middle East*. Berkeley, CA: University of California Press.

Zubaida, S. (2001) "Civil Society, Community and Democracy in the Middle East" in S. Kaviraj and S. Khilnani (eds) *Civil Society: History and Possibilities*. Cambridge: Cambridge University Press.

Zubaida, S. (2001/2) "Islam and the Politics of Citizenship and Community," *Middle East Report*, no. 221, Winter.

Zubaida, S. (2002) "The Fragments Imagine the Nation: the Case of Iraq," *International Journal of Middle East Studies*, 34(2).

Zubaida, S. (1993) *Islam, the People and the State*. London: I.B. Tauris.

Zubaida, S. (2003) *Law and Power in the Islamic World*. London: I.B. Tauris.

Index

www.ingramcontent.com/pod-product-compliance
Ingram Content Group UK Ltd.
Pitfield, Milton Keynes, MK11 3LW, UK
UKHW020415010325
455677UK00029B/896